THE HIGHLY SENSITIVE PERSON

Building Social Relationships and Emotional Intelligence as an HSP - How to Overcome Anxiety and Worry and Stop Emotional Overload with EQ Strategies

THE HIGHLY SENSITIVE PERSON

© Copyright 2020 - **All rights reserved.**

The content contained within this book may not be reproduced, duplicated or transmitted without direct written permission from the author or the publisher.

Under no circumstances will any blame or legal responsibility be held against the publisher, or author, for any damages, reparation, or monetary loss due to the information contained within this book, either directly or indirectly.

Legal Notice:

This book is copyright protected. It is only for personal use. You cannot amend, distribute, sell, use, quote or paraphrase any part, or the content within this book, without the consent of the author or publisher.

Disclaimer Notice:

Please note the information contained within this document is for educational and entertainment purposes only. All effort has been executed to present accurate, up to date, reliable, complete information. No warranties of any kind are declared or implied. Readers acknowledge that the author is not engaged in the rendering of legal, financial, medical or professional advice. The content within this book has been derived from various sources. Please consult a licensed professional before attempting any techniques outlined in this book.

By reading this document, the reader agrees that under no circumstances is the author responsible for any losses, direct or indirect, that are incurred as a result of the use of the information contained within this document, including, but not limited to, errors, omissions, or inaccuracies.

THE HIGHLY SENSITIVE PERSON

Building Social Relationships and Emotional Intelligence as an HSP - How to Overcome Anxiety and Worry and Stop Emotional Overload with EQ Strategies

ADDISON BELL

Table of Contents

Introduction 9
   Introducing Highly Sensitive Persons 12
Chapter 1: Understanding the Highly Sensitive Person ... 20
   Sensitivity to Diet 21
   Sensitivity to Environment 22
   Sensitivity to Stimulation 23
   Sensitivity to Emotions 23
   The Highly Sensitive Child (HSC) and Discipline 26
   Orchids and Dandelions 32
   Shutting Out the Noise 37
   Provide Structure 39
   Ruling on Rumination 40
Chapter 2: What it Feels Like Being an HSP 43
   Ramblings of an HSP Newborn 44
   A Mother's Love 53
   Patrick's Perspective 59
Chapter 3: High Sensitivity in an Insensitive World 63
   External Overload 78
   Recognize Emotional Irritants 80
   Internal Peace and Calm 82
Chapter 4: The Highly Sensitive Person's Gifts to the World 85
   Strengths 90

Limitations 92
All About Abby 93

Chapter 5: HSPs and Emotional Intelligence 110
What Makes Emotional Intelligence So Important? 113
Differences Between IQ and EQ 119
Mayer and Salovey Method of Emotional Intelligence. 121
Highly Sensitive People and Emotional Intelligence..... 125

Chapter 6: EQ Awareness Strategies 130
Becoming More Self-Aware 130
Becoming More Socially Aware 138

Chapter 7: EQ Management Strategies 151
How to Master Self-Management 151
Mastering Relationship Management 163

Chapter 8: Anxiety and the Highly Sensitive Person 173
Dealing with Anxiety as an HSP 174
Routines Provide Structure 179
Overcoming Anxiety with Emotional Intelligence........ 182

Chapter 9: Worry and the Highly Sensitive Person 195
Worry as a Highly Sensitive Person 196
Overcoming Worry Using Emotional Intelligence 202
Self-Awareness 211
Self-Regulation 212
Social Awareness and Management 214

Chapter 10: Emotional Overload as an HSP 217
Emotional Overload as an HSP 218
How Does it Feel to be Overstimulated? 228
Conventional Ways of Overcoming Overwhelm 232

 Overcoming Emotional Overload Using Emotional
  Intelligence 234
**Chapter 11: HSP Relationships Using Emotional
Intelligence 241**
 HSPs and Relationships 241
 HSPs and Emotions in Relationships 245
 HSPs and Non-Sensitives 251
Conclusion 260
References 267

Introduction

"Highly sensitive beings suffer more but they also love harder, dream wider and experience deeper horizons and bliss. When you're sensitive, you're alive in every sense of this word in this wildly beautiful world. Sensitivity is your strength. Keep soaking in the light and spreading it to others."
~ Victoria Erickson

My very first exposure to emotional intelligence, also known as EQ, was way back in 2010 when I was invited to attend a presentation to learn about how various personalities interact with one another as well as the difference between them. This would take me on a fascinating journey over the next decade, meeting with people from all walks of life, age groups, ethnicity, and genders. What I was mostly involved with was identifying what makes people do the things they do, and the motivation behind the decisions they make.

Let's rewind to the first time I learned all about emotional intelligence. The presentation was given by a visiting psychologist, author, and founder of an emotional intelligence testing modality that's exceptionally accurate and fun to engage. Meeting with this psychologist was revolutionary for my spouse and I because it wasn't even a few minutes into his presentation where I could immediately identify my husband as being a personality type that was completely opposite to mine. It turns out that he is a Highly Sensitive Person (HSP). This is not a term that is used in this form of personality profiling, but it has been something I've had to discover by searching through various books and a decade's worth of research.

Part of this system involves understanding each of the different personalities, what makes them unique, and how to interact with them successfully. This was to be the beginning of a journey of discovery for me. It was fascinating discovering what makes people do the things they do and what the main motivation behind these choices and decisions are. One of the first lessons learned from this presentation was that while my husband and I are highly compatible, we are at opposite ends of a spectrum. I discovered that the way I've been dealing with people all along has been wrong. I am possibly what you might call the least sensitive individual on the planet. I don't flap, get flustered, or have mood fluctuations. Instead, my temperament is fairly even and straightforward. I make decisions quickly and until that point, I had expected the same from everyone around me.

It was only at this presentation that I was horrified to discover how very wrong I had been. All along, I was pressuring my husband when it came to making decisions. I couldn't understand why he would constantly drag his heels... After all, what was so difficult about making a simple decision? Quite frankly, I am the type of person who makes decisions at the drop of a hat. If it turns out to be the wrong decision, I will simply move onto option B, C, D, or E, as those alternate choices were already in the back of my mind.

My husband, on the other hand, needed to be left to ruminate, weigh up all the pros and cons, and finally decide only when he was 100% comfortable that his decision was the very best of all available options. Here, I had been placing him under much more pressure than necessary, and giving myself ulcers in the process because I was totally frustrated by his inability to come up with a simple decision.

As we continued to listen to the psychologist describe each of the personality traits that could be found within each of the unique groups, I was more convinced than ever that I needed to change the way that I was communicating with my husband. I realized how extremely important it was to learn as much as I possibly could about emotional intelligence and how it could be used to strengthen relationships, no matter how difficult people could seem.

Would it be challenging? You bet! Would it be worth it? Absolutely!

Introducing Highly Sensitive Persons

If you or a loved one have ever been told, "You're way too sensitive!" you probably wished that you could find some magic remedy to make you feel normal, to be just like everybody else. But suppose that wish was the very thing that was stopping you from achieving that dream of being who you're really meant to be? There's actually nothing wrong with you. You are what is known as a Highly Sensitive Person or an HSP. The Highly Sensitive Person is also sometimes known as someone who has sensory processing sensitivity (SPS). This is a personality characteristic where the individual has "an increased sensitivity of the central nervous system and a deeper cognitive processing of physical, social, and emotional stimuli" (Boterberg & Warreyn, 2016).

What if this person is already inside you, just waiting to be set free on the world with some coping mechanisms that could make all the difference? Of course, the coping mechanisms I'm referring to are those associated with emotional intelligence, or EQ. I'd like to share with you some of the lessons I've learned so far regarding how emotional intelligence can successfully be applied in the life of a Highly Sensitive Person.

This may be the first time you've ever heard of the term Highly Sensitive Person (HSP), and you may have a lot of questions that you'd like answered. This book may provide you with some of the answers that you've been looking for, especially when you have been feeling highly emotional about the world around you. How will you get a definitive answer about whether you are an HSP or not? There are some clues to know whether you fall into this unique and relatively small percentage of individuals in the world today who are HSPs.

Although I mentioned that the percentage of Highly Sensitive Persons is small, they actually make up approximately 20% of the world's total population. It's been confirmed that the total is equal to more than the total population of China. This statistic should make you feel much better knowing that you're not alone, having to deal with your emotions. You're not a freak of nature, or broken, and no, you don't need to force yourself to fit into a specific mold.

You shouldn't need to be told how to act or react under certain circumstances. While you may not enjoy some of the common characteristics that make up a Highly Sensitive Person's personality, hopefully you will come to realize that each of these traits is necessary in the world today. You may be asking yourself the following questions:

- What does a typical Highly Sensitive Person look like?
- Was I born this way, or did something happen to me in my past to make me like this?
- How do I get over this condition?
- I hate feeling overstimulated all the time; what can I do about it?

- I'm really selective when it comes to relationships with people; is this normal?
- Why did I find school so challenging?
- I battle to contain my emotions and usually end up crying hopelessly.
- People seem to treat me differently and this makes me feel worse.
- I really battle to form close personal relationships with others.
- Is there something I can do to feel less overwhelmed by sights and sounds?
- People treat me like I'm an *agony aunt*—whenever they have problems, they seem to rely on me. I don't enjoy it, but I also don't want to hurt their feelings.
- I hate it when people tell me to just "toughen up, and get over it" – how do I deal with these people?
- Is it normal and natural for me to not enjoy change? I am comfortable with things just the way they are.
- Is it normal to feel so overly sensitive to everything around me, even to the clothes I wear?

- Is it normal for me to live in constant fear of rejection?
- My brain and mind constantly seem to be overstimulated. What can I do to get this under control?
- How can I tell my friends that I would prefer to stay at home, rather than facing crowds, without hurting their feelings?
- Why do I feel so much more deeply than everyone around me?
- I am constantly worrying about things and this is leading to feelings of anxiety and depression.
- How do I get off this emotional rollercoaster that I've been on my entire life?

I want you to know that you are not the only one searching for the answers to these questions. Helping you to discover the answer to these questions is the reason for this publication. These are just some of the questions that we'll be addressing in the chapters that follow. We will consider where you fall on the emotional intelligence spectrum and how to use emotional intelligence techniques to help you to cope with your feelings.

Emotional intelligence is all about learning how to connect with others and deal with those that are completely different from you. If you happen to fall into the 20% Highly Sensitive Person spectrum, there is going to be another 80% of the world that you will need to learn how to deal with in order to not only survive, but to thrive.

In *The Highly Sensitive Person: Building Social Relationships and EQ as an HSP – How to Overcome Anxiety and Worry and Stop Emotional Overload with EQ Strategies*, it is my goal to provide you with all the tools that you need to function in every area of your life, without all the fear and anxiety that you may be used to having. I'm here to reassure you that, from the very start of this journey, I will be with you every step of the way.

I'm not here to turn your entire life upside down or on its head; my whole aim is to make your life easier. The aim is to make your relationships easier, and to release some of the stress and anxiety you may be experiencing while trying to confirm to a society that is largely different to who you are. This is here to help you on this journey, so that you can discover the secrets to thriving, rather than merely surviving, and feel better every day.

I'm also not going to make a promise that these changes are going to be comfortable or easy. In fact, nothing worthwhile having in life ever is easy. The beauty of this is that you have a choice to make. You can keep doing what you've been doing as a Highly Sensitive Person, or the parent, boss, employee, child, spouse, or significant other of someone who is a Highly Sensitive Person. In many instances, we become so set in our ways, and yes, even HSPs do this, that we cannot recognize the value in making changes in our lives.

The goal is to empower you with all of the tools and skills that you'll need to be effective, well-balanced, happy, and a contributing member of society. There are already many skills and talents that Highly Sensitive Persons can share with the world. It needs to be stated right at the beginning of this book that the world desperately needs all types of people. This includes those who are sensitive to everything in the world around them and those who continue to function regardless of what's happening. This latter description refers to the non-sensitive 80% of the population of the world.

Join me as we discover what makes each Highly Sensitive Person unique in their own right. Discover the wonderful gifts that they bring to the world, how their gifts and abilities can be harnessed and celebrated for what they are, and what they bring to the world. While there are certain areas within emotional intelligence that need to be finetuned, there are other areas where an HSP has better interpersonal and intrapersonal skills, making them highly effective at certain emotional intelligence strategies, while leaving them wanting by others. By the end of this journey, you should have all the tools necessary to move boldly through life, especially if you're an HSP. You will be adept at toning down some of the overstimulation that occurs in the life of every Highly Sensitive Person, as well as effectively dealing with the multitude of emotions that seem to bombard you from every possible angle.

In *The Highly Sensitive Person: Building Social Relationships and EQ as an HSP – How to Overcome Anxiety and Worry and Stop Emotional Overload with EQ Strategies*, we will work with a two-pronged approach; one from the perspective of a Highly Sensitive Person and the second from someone trying to navigate the sometimes choppy waters. If you are an HSP, you have probably been told that you possess many unique gifts that you can bless the world with. It's our intention to highlight each of these gifts so you can maximize their influence in your life.

Chapter 1:
Understanding the Highly Sensitive Person

In his book, *Divine Living: The Essential Guide to Your True Destiny*, author, Anthon St. Maarten, had the following to say about Highly Sensitive Persons:

> *"To feel intensely is not a symptom of weakness... Highly sensitive people are often perceived as weaklings or damaged goods. To feel intensely is not a symptom of weakness, it is the trademark of the truly alive and compassionate. It is not the empath who is broken, it is society that has become dysfunctional and emotionally disabled. There is no shame expressing your authentic feelings. Those who are at times described as being a 'hot mess' or having 'too many issues' are the very fabric of what keeps the dream alive for a more caring, humane world. Never be afraid to let your tears shine a light in this world."*

From the time that a Highly Sensitive Person is born, they are immediately hit with an overload of stimuli. With anything from bright or flashing lights to loud noises around them, a baby HSP really battles to keep it all together. They're never referred to as an easy baby! If this describes your baby, you are about to begin your worst nightmare as a parent, unless you're also an HSP, in which case you're likely to feed off of one another's emotions causing a unique form of chaos.

HSP babies are distinct in the sense that they possess some very distinct character traits that set them apart from other babies. Some of these traits include, but aren't limited to:

Sensitivity to Diet

The HSP baby is sensitive to the mother's diet if she is breastfeeding. There's a possibility that they may have food allergies which causes them to spit up a lot or they may be a colicky baby, with increased gas. By the time the baby starts eating soft foods, even the texture of the food being offered may prove to be too much. Instead, they prefer to weigh their options about deciding to even taste that orange stuff you have on the end of the spoon, no matter how many cooing noises or "choo choo" trains you add into the equation.

Sensitivity to Environment

Although, these babies will battle to quieten themselves without calming reassurance and a soft voice, they prefer to have someone around to do so. Laundry detergents, baby wipes, other cleaning products, and chemicals could cause adverse skin reactions in these babies.

They are definitely more temperature sensitive and need to be given a lot of love and affection. They battle to acclimatize to different temperatures. They need to know that they are loved and be held by members of their family. They prefer adults who have softer, melodic voices, rather than hard, stern or gruff ones. They are likely to develop allergic reactions to all sorts of things. In their environment, they are prone to developing skin rashes depending on where they are. This could be due to allergic reactions to the environment and/or skin sensitivity. In babyhood, this might include things like tags and seams on clothing, various textures such as wool, and/or synthetics. They could become totally iffy whenever they are dirty, wet or sticky, which, let's face it with a baby, is pretty often. These babies often suffer from separation anxiety, and won't easily go to others, especially strangers.

Sensitivity to Stimulation

When it comes to overstimulation, they don't like lots of people around them, and will often cry or throw tantrums when they are older. Loud noises frighten or disturb them. On the plus side, they are generally ahead of the curve when it comes to speech and development. These babies pick things up super-fast, making them inquisitive in their surroundings. They are quick to pick things up that are happening around them. These babies may be more sensitive than others when it comes to sleep as well. They could sleep very lightly or require additional soothing before being put down.

Sensitivity to Emotions

For the HSP baby, your emotions are amplified 1,000-fold. As a brand-new mom, you dare not battle with postpartum depression or get freaked out because you find the whole parenting thing to be overwhelming. Baby will pick up even the slightest cue that your body is sending and will amplify these emotions right back at you! So, how can you successfully deal with a highly sensitive baby effectively? The first thing you need to do is to take care of yourself. It's going to be your responsibility to center and balance your own emotions, so that you can be as calm as a cucumber with your child. Read as many books and blogs as you can about Highly Sensitive Persons to gain as much information as possible. There are YouTube videos, podcasts, and many scientific studies that can provide you with the information you seek. It's understanding the difference between an HSP and a non-sensitive child that will put things into perspective for you.

As a parent, your main responsibility or goal in life should be to provide the best possible environment for your child. There are support groups on Facebook that you can join for further advice and encouragement. One of the best ways to gain further insight is by finding other parents or individuals who are going through what you are (Bjelland, n.d.).

Founder of the term, "Highly Sensitive Person," Elaine Aron, describes Highly Sensitive Children as being either super-difficult, or almost too easy to raise. Because they form part of the 15% to 20% of Highly Sensitive Persons born, they possess a nervous system that's making them extremely aware of everything going on around them one hundred percent of the time. Because of this, they pick up on the finer nuances of absolutely everything. Instead of lashing out in reaction to a situation, they're more inclined to spend some time reflecting on the situation before taking action. They're usually extremely conscientious.

Should their surroundings be highly stimulating, they are inclined to become overwhelmed by the slightest change in environment. They pick up on the emotional stress that others may be feeling, absorbing this stress within themselves. Aron states that children often possess a unique blend of several traits and this makes certain Highly Sensitive Children extremely difficult to raise because they're emotionally intense. On the other hand, there are those who are extremely calm, and easy to raise because they are shyer and more reserved than those at the opposite end of the Highly Sensitive Person spectrum. Both of these types of children will usually have issues when they are forced to play with a group of children whom they don't know. Elaine Aron reiterates that whichever side of the highly sensitive spectrum your child falls on, they are both going to be extremely sensitive to their environments (physical, and emotional).

The Highly Sensitive Child (HSC) and Discipline

For healthy children, discipline is an important component of parenting. While this may be difficult with non-sensitive children, trying to discipline a sensitive child will seem like an uphill battle because they are far more susceptible to emotions than other children. Here are some guidelines for disciplining this kind of child:

First and foremost, there's nothing wrong with being sensitive. The child is not abnormal, defective, or broken (like some people believe). In most instances, these children are the most caring, compassionate, empathetic, and kindest children you will ever meet. Before you can begin to discipline them, there are a couple of things you need to know.

These children get overwhelmed in tense situations and you may find yourself with a child pouring their heart out to you between sobs. Because they feel things so deeply, they worry unnecessarily. Remember that, with these children, everything is amplified. That means that when they're sad, they're really extremely emotional. When they're feeling hurt, it cuts them deeply. They feel these emotions on a much deeper scale than their non-sensitive counterparts. As if being emotionally sensitive isn't enough for these children, many of them are hypersensitive when it comes to stimuli. Anything from bright lights to loud noises and even certain textures can set them off. For many of these children, being among too many people is simply too much for them to handle and they prefer sticking with a rigid routine rather than having to try and deal with change (Pluess et al., 2018).

Some of the biggest challenges facing Highly Sensitive Children are their peers. They often get saddled with labels that stick with them much longer than necessary, causing them to become even more frustrated with their lives. Non-sensitive kids can easily do the whole punishment thing and often come out better for it. For a Highly Sensitive Child, punishment is more likely to cause further problems. These kids often need a completely different approach, versus their non-sensitive opposites. Here are some suggestions from psychotherapist, Editor-in-Chief of Verywell Mind, and author and host of the *Mentally Strong People* podcast, Amy Morin:

Apply Logical Outcomes

When disciplining your Highly Sensitive Child, you need to be able to be firm, but fair. They must understand that when they've done something wrong, there are certain outcomes attached to the behavior. Be sure that you apply logical reasoning to each of these outcomes rather than focusing on disciplining the child. It should be more about what makes logical sense, so the HSC can understand the *why* behind the behavior. This is a life lesson that all children deserve to be taught. When working with your HSC, speak in calm tones, so that you don't set them off.

Compliment Their Hard Work
Compliment your child each time they do something that is praiseworthy. HSCs need more encouragement than non-sensitive children do. From a psychological perspective, this praise and encouragement can help to build self-esteem. One of the most important things regarding this would be to ensure that you are praising them each time that the praise is earned, rather than simply praising them for the sake of stroking. It's important, according to Morin, that the effort be praised rather than the outcome.

Educate Them to Solve Their Problems
This refers to getting them past the stage of feeling so completely overwhelmed that they begin to feel anxiety and stress. Highly Sensitive Children need a process that

they can follow whenever there is a problem directly in front of them. This will often be the difference between experiencing high levels of anxiety and having the self-confidence needed to push through a situation.

Establish Boundaries

Just as you would for your other children, your HSC needs to know that there are boundaries in place when it comes to acceptable behavior. You are already giving your HSC plenty of leeway, so beware that they don't make an excuse for this to become a habit. You have to appreciate how important discipline is for all children because it will ultimately prepare them to face the challenges of life in the future. Through discipline, your Highly Sensitive Child is also able to discover for themselves that actions have consequences and this gives them opportunities to grow.

Explain Feeling Phrases

HSCs are constantly feeling emotions, absorbing whatever emotions happen to be floating around at the time (including those of others). It's important for them to be able to communicate exactly how they are feeling, rather than bottling the emotions inside. As a parent of an HSC, guide them by teaching them words that they can use to describe what they are feeling, while they are feeling them. This is an important communication tool.

Extend Quiet Time

For the Highly Sensitive Child, just getting through the day can be extremely challenging. Remember how they feel dealing with crowds. They could easily find school and other activities draining because they're constantly being overstimulated by what's happening around them. Be sure that there's a quiet space where they can withdraw to in order to unwind after a busy day. This space should ultimately just be for them, without allowing other siblings to gatecrash and upset their mood further. Morin shares some ideas regarding headphones with some relaxing music, books to read, and anything that will allow them to destress.

Present Incentives

For the HSC, they view almost their entire lives as being close to getting into trouble. Their peers always seem to judge them and shun them for being different. They are so hypersensitive that even when a situation has nothing to do with them, they automatically assume that people are discussing them. They feel like failures and have to prove themselves to everyone, all the time. When it comes to offering an incentive for doing something, carefully consider the way that you frame the initial incentive. Choose your words specifically so that they feel that they'd like to make an attempt at earning the incentive. If they don't quite succeed, encourage them to try again another day, rather than simply rewarding them in any event.

Understand Their Sensitivity
If you are aware that you have a Highly Sensitive Child, accept them for who and what they are. Don't try to force them to conform to a specific mold that you may hold for your other, non-sensitive children. Acknowledge that they are different, without making them feel uncomfortable about it. Remember that they are able to pick up on every single emotion that you're giving off. Recognize their strengths and their weaknesses. You also don't want to be wrapping them up in bubble wrap, but you should try not to force them to do things that make them feel uncomfortable. It's easy to become frustrated, so just be sure that you're not setting out those vibes, rather than ones of acceptance and love, just for who they are (Morin & Lockhart, 2020).

Orchids and Dandelions

Professor Thomas Boyce, from the University of California, was the first to categorize two different types of children, the first of which is orchid children who have very specific needs and requirements while growing up. They need to be tended and nurtured more than their dandelion counterparts. Stop and think about how very different each of these flowers is from one another. Once again, you get an exquisitely delicate plant that only flowers under exactly the right circumstances. It needs to be located in exactly the right place, with the right amount of light, with either a drip or mist irrigation system, or in a steamy environment such as close to a hot tub or in a bathroom. Once you know all the how's, where's, and why's about taking care of your orchid, they seem to be able to thrive. They are still pretty finicky though and don't do well with changes to their environment. You can't have them south-facing on one day and suddenly move them to a west-facing view the next. The outcome is surely going to be one where the orchid withers and dies.

Only occasionally are they able to flower again when the season and conditions are just right for them, but they still need to be tended just as you would if they were still flowering. You cannot give them too much water because the roots would soon become water-logged and stifled. Under-watering, on the other hand, hardens the outside layer of the stalk, preventing all the necessary nutrients from reaching these delicate flowers. They cannot be coaxed into flowering by placing them under unnatural conditions. They, like most exotic plants, will wither and die.

Next to these beautiful, delicate blooms with such distinguishing yet fragile features, the dandelion is a stark contrast. They literally bloom anywhere and everywhere, even coming through cracks in sidewalks or in the road. For them, it's all the same—all they need is a tiny bit of soil and for their parachute seedlings to be germinated. Dandelions are classified as weeds, yet they can have such a profound effect all standing tall on long stems, waiting for their turn to transform. If you've ever had the privilege of watching a child, any child, play with dandelions that have turned, you will know how they love to blow them and watch each tiny parachute float gradually down until they nestle gently on the grass, or find a minute patch of sand. This will become their new home.

Dandelions don't need anything to survive and thrive other than some grass, a little bit of soil, some water and sunlight. When the weather is overcast, they close their buds (similar to the way that sunflowers droop), however, once the sun is out again, a carpet of small brightly colored golden flowers will span the fields. Even in crags of rocks or sidewalks, roads or concrete, wherever dandelions find a place to land and germinate, they will come up resilient and hardy as ever.

What do each of these plants have to do with Highly Sensitive Persons or Highly Sensitive Children? It's quite simple. The differentiators between these two plants are environment, nurturing, and resilience. For anyone who's ever owned or tended an orchid, no matter the variety, you will know that they are high maintenance plants. You have to give them just the right amount of sunlight. They prefer to be sprayed infrequently with water. Orchids fare so much better when they have a combination of treebark and mulch, rather than potting soil. This, of course, has something to do with the bark's ability to hold water, rather than looking esthetically pleasing.

Similarly, an HSC needs a lot more attention and care than their dandelion counterparts.

Dandelions are hardy and resilient. They don't need much to survive and thrive, even in some of the most challenging conditions. Through decades of study by clinical and research pediatricians and other psychologists, they are only now beginning to understand the differences between these two distinct types of individuals. Where 15% to 20% of the world's population will fall into the orchid category, the balance all fall within the dandelion spectrum. Yet, both are necessary for the other to survive. It's important to understand how both think and process information in order for you to be able to work with them effectively.

In a number of lectures given on the subject of these two types of children, Professor Boyce describes how he and his sister grew up in the same home, under exactly the same set of circumstances, where they were treated in the same way, and raised with the same set of standards or rules. Boyce explains that he went on to medical school, has been in the same stable marriage for more than 40 years, and describes his life as being almost idyllic. His sister, only a couple of years younger than he, developed some debilitating illnesses while she was quite young, was diagnosed as a schizophrenic by the time she was 20, and fell pregnant in college and gave birth to a child who was badly deformed. His sister found the only solution to all of life's problems was choosing to commit suicide at age 52.

For years, Boyce could not understand how there could be such a completely different outcome between two siblings raised under identical circumstances. How could their lives turn out to be so completely different? He now understands that while he was a dandelion child, his sister Mary was actually an orchid child and needed much more love and nurturing than he required. Growing up in the 1950's, everyone was treated exactly the same way. The only thing that set people apart was class distinction, the haves versus the have-nots. It was even implied during early research into this phenomenon that socioeconomic backgrounds were the only contributing factor. If you came from a poor environment, you would likely end up falling within the group more susceptible to being resilient, and being able to overcome just about anything that the world could throw your way.

Further studies were conducted in a controlled environment where children were brought in and asked a series of questions or challenges (some of them designed to raise stress levels). Apart from sitting with a mental health practitioner who was able to assist if necessary, it was the first time that brain activity was being measured for specific fluctuations or changes. The results were interesting. It was discovered that approximately 80% of those assessed showed the same curve where there was very little to almost no movement above or below the mean average. The other 20% showed extreme fluctuations as they were under pressure during certain test modalities. This provided further proof that this 20% of those tested were actually HSC and there was little to substantiate previous claims that socioeconomic backgrounds had anything to do with it (Boyce, 2019).

Shutting Out the Noise

For an HSP, they are on high alert 24/7 and nothing ever shuts down completely. That includes the never-ending droning monologues that you continue to have with yourself. This self-talk is one of the more common characteristics of someone who is a Highly Sensitive Person. The self-talk could virtually be about anything, from trying to remember where you put the car keys while you're already running late, to mentally checking and rechecking whether you happened to close and lock all of the windows in your home because there's been a weather report and you realize that you are right in the middle of its projected path.

As a Highly Sensitive Person, there are a couple of things that you do completely differently to everyone else. Your mind is constantly in process mode. Accept it because it's innate. This means that it's something that you were born with. It makes up the very fabric of your DNA and who you are. There is absolutely nothing you can do to change it, so why not celebrate your unique gifts and move on? While your brain seems to be working overtime, it has the capacity to understand what's going through it and so it's not just some wild ramblings that are all garbled.

This is why Highly Sensitive Children need to be stimulated mentally from the time they are really young. They have inquisitive minds. They want to know how things work.

You're most likely to walk into the house where there are several appliances or things that function mechanically that have been meticulously pulled apart in an attempt to discover exactly how they work. Chances are, they will be able to put the items back together again unharmed. As a parent of an HSC, you may want to invest in some educational games and toys from a young age that will challenge your child's intellect and allow them to discover things for themselves through exploration. The amazing thing about our world today is that this is no longer just a category that would be left to boys. There are some pretty bright girls in the world who are just as capable of making it when it comes to mechanical engineering, design, and various other technical vocations.

Provide Structure

Any HSP needs a degree of normality and structure for their day and their time. Did I mention that they don't like change at all? If you need to change something with them it's best that you sit down and explain things to them logically. This is exactly how a Highly Sensitive Person thinks. They prefer to weigh the pros and cons of a situation, rather than simply just jumping in with both feet—they leave that to their non-sensitive counterparts. The more structure your HSP has, the better for everyone. If you have a blended family where there is more than one child, it's best to hold a family meeting so that everyone understands the ground rules. This will serve to create a safe space for your Highly Sensitive Child to thrive in when it comes to being within the walls of your own home.

Ruling on Rumination

About all that self-talk that keeps happening in the mind of an HSC, most of the time, the talk is pretty negative. It's also cyclic, meaning that there seems to be no beginning or end of the thought process, it just is. From a psychological perspective, if you had a start or end point for your rumination, it would be much easier to identify what was triggering it and working on this instead.

Watch out for negative thoughts taking up space in the head. Try and figure out what's causing them so that you can get them under control as a matter of urgency. By not doing so, what was once a small molehill, can turn into an enormous mountain, especially for a Highly Sensitive Person. Think for a moment of all of the different emotions that are leaning toward the negative side. As an HSP, you feel *all* of these emotions more intensely than anyone else. When you're feeling sad, you feel a deep, gut-wrenching, soul-destroying sorrow, rather than just sadness. You can physically feel it to your very core. At the other end of the spectrum, if you were happy, the feelings of joy, happiness, elation, bliss, and euphoria would be hard for you to contain.

If you know that you're prone to your mind wandering off, try some of the following techniques to keep yourself grounded in the here and now, rather than being transported back into the past and reliving things that have already happened. Because a Highly Sensitive Person feels things much more intensely than a non-sensitive individual, they are likely to hold grudges longer and replay scenarios over and over in the mind, trying to see if things could have possibly played out differently. In a sense, a Highly Sensitive Person places themselves into a state of high alert and high stress because of things they imagine in their heads, rather than what is actually happening.

Dr. Jadzia Jagiellowicz is a research scientist who specializes in working with Highly Sensitive Persons. Many of her scientific studies and papers have been completed in conjunction with both Drs. Elaine and Art Aron. At the moment, she is working closely as a professional coach to HSPs. According to Dr. Jagiellowicz, "Highly sensitive people are biologically predisposed to react more strongly to their environment, including having more intense negative thoughts (Jagiellowicz, 2019).

Jagiellowicz warns that as long as your brain continues to ruminate over the past, it's attempting to come up with a solution to whatever the problem is. It will continue to do so indefinitely, unless you find a way to break these thought patterns (McLaughlin & Hoeksema, 2010).

One of the most important messages that you can take away from this first chapter is that there's nothing broken or bent out of shape with someone who is a Highly Sensitive Person. Instead, they have been born with some unique gifts that they bring to the world. They are extremely intuitive and feel things on a level that non-sensitive people will probably never be able to comprehend. If you have just discovered that you or a loved one are an HSP, then your journey is just beginning. Let's be sure that you're giving yourself the time to process things as you need to. You are beautiful and special and have many gifts and talents to bring to this crazy world. Let's discover some of these gifts and talents together.

Chapter 2:
What it Feels Like Being an HSP

"They hear nearly every sound, notice every movement, and process the expression on every person's face. And that means that simply walking through a public place can be an assault on their senses."
~ Andre Sólo

From the moment the HSP child is born, everything around them is heightened and amplified. From the bright lights of the theatre where they first come into this world, to all of the expressions on people's faces, they immediately begin reading all the tiny cues written there and listening to the inflection in the various voices. Perhaps it's a good thing that newborns can't talk immediately. This may give you some insight as to how a brand new HSC is thinking and processing everything that begins at the time they enter this world. I've taken a bit of creative and poetic license to voice the way that possible monologues would go:

The Highly Sensitive Person

Ramblings of an HSP Newborn

"Ah, that's a soothing voice that's calm and loving. This voice I will come to know and recognize as that of my Mother. My father's voice is a little less soft, but I can tell that there's love behind the words." These are probably some of the first thoughts that will run through your highly sensitive baby's head, right from when they're born. They already know that they need to process everything… and in return, communicate in the only way they understand how to at that moment, by screaming loudly! Future thoughts will ensue as in, "I'm hungry, I don't like the way this stickiness feels in my nappy, get it off of me and quickly… Being in a bath is soothing on my skin, but the temperature must be just right, or I get easily startled. I will show you exactly what I mean by startled. Don't worry mother, we've got this—together we can do this, as long as you stay closely in tune with the signals I'll give you."

"Pay close attention now because I'm nothing like the other children who are coming and pressing their faces too close to mine right now! They frighten me when they do that! I'm going to let you know that I don't really like it very much, I want you to pick me up and protect me from them, so I'm going to let out a loud yell. Please don't be angry with me. I'm trying to let you know what's working for me right now and what's not!"

"The tag on the back of whatever you've dressed me in is chafing the back of my neck. It's irritating me... get it off me and now! No! I'm not hungry and I don't need changing yet. I'm not running a fever. Keep going, and eventually you'll notice a red mark beginning to appear at the base of my neck. It doesn't hurt as bad when you put me on my tummy. But I really would prefer wearing something that won't irritate me so."

"Yawn... I'm actually so tired, but there's too much noise around me to sleep. Too many different people are all cooing and wanting to hold me... I don't like this very much because I don't know them. Mother, please take me back and keep me safe with you. Your voice can soothe away any of my stressful emotions right now. Maybe I will even be able to fall asleep because I feel safe in your arms. What was that loud noise? More people! Don't they know that Mother and I are both tired and would like to sleep? It's bad enough that the people you refer to as 'nurses' and 'doctors' are already poking and prodding me all the time. All I want is to be able to sleep for longer than a few minutes at a time."

"That loud ringing is hurting my ears, so I cry! It takes Mother a while to rock me back to a place where I feel calm and content again. All the people seem to be leaving, so maybe we will finally be able to have some alone time with just Mother, Father and me. I'd like to spend some time with my father where he holds me too. I need to get used to the sound of his voice. He also sounds fairly gentle and has a calming effect over me. He will be my protector for the first few years of my life. This is why I need to develop a bond with him as soon as possible. His skin is not as soft as Mother's, but I feel safe being supported by his strong grip. He has a special smell that I don't really mind."

"It's bath time again? Maybe you'll see the mark from my little t-shirt on the back of my neck now and try to figure out some way to stop these from hurting me so. The towel that you have me sitting on is plush at first, but don't press too hard with it."

"Woah, not so much of that smelly stuff in the water— I'm not sure how my skin is going to react to it. You're getting the hang of this; the temperature of the water is almost just right today. I only cried once while you bathed me and that was when I got a fright as you turned me over. I thought you were going to drop me. Sorry if I startled you, but you should have seen it from my perspective! All these faces again, poking and prodding me every few minutes."

"What does it mean to be 'jaundiced?' I'm going to have to be here in the hospital longer? How much longer? And you're going to put me into one of those hot box things, except this time there are purple lights? I briefly saw these when one of the things you covered my eyes with came loose. It's nice and warm in there, but I don't feel comfortable without my clothes on! Mother, are you there? I can't hear you or see anything… there's just a gentle hum of this box that I'm in. Please come back, I need to hold your finger, even if it's just for a while. I'm scared! I don't like it here anymore."

"Why do they keep on pricking my foot… it hurts when they squeeze it—I'm going to let out a loud yell so that hopefully you will come and rescue me from these people. Thank you for getting me out of there when you did, even if it was just to feed me. I can recognize the way you smell, Mother, and know that you will always do whatever you can to keep me safe. As for the rest of these people, why is the doctor looking so stern? What do the pieces of paper in his hands tell him about what's happening to me? I really don't want to go back into the box. Promise me that you will come and hold my hand until I fall asleep. Thank you for putting a beanie on my head, I was beginning to feel a little chilly being in a space this big with only my nappy on. Yawn... hopefully I can get some sleep! Mother, don't you leave me now, I still have my hand clenching one of your fingers tightly."

"So, it's way too bright out here after you've removed the protection over my eyes. I preferred the low light that was around a few hours ago. Whatever you're wrapping me in now is really soft and gentle against my skin. I like it! Where's 'home?' Why are all these people "oohing and aahing" over me? Can we just get out of here now? This has been an emotional rollercoaster for me since I got here! What's this funny shaped thing you're strapping me into? It's stopping me from moving my head side to side, as well as my arms and legs. I don't know how I feel about this yet. Although it does feel quite safe and secure, like before I came into this place. Mother, why are you crying? Have I done something wrong? Is there a way for me to fix how you're feeling right now, because I can sense that your emotions are all up in the air! Okay, I'm going to have a good long cry with you. Let's see if we can figure this out together shall we?"

"We're on the move. I still feel very safe and secure in this thing that you're calling a "baby car seat," but as we begin heading out, everything is really, really bright. Close me up, I don't like the bright lights so much. There's also a cool breeze blowing that's making me feel slightly chilly. Thank you, that's much better. This space feels snug and warmer now. Why are you stopping and what's that beeping sound? It's hurting my ears. Okay, thank you—now it's gone. It feels like we're in a bigger space than the warm box I was in. I can hear clicking noises and my chair is no longer moving. Father is helping Mother get into the car. She sounds exhausted and emotional at the same time. Did I make her feel like this? It's my fault. I think I'm going to cry!"

"Hold on, what's that purring sound? That sounds similar to the noise I heard in the box with the lights, but much louder. There's a slight beeping and clicking and then a smooth ride for quite a while—Yawn, this is so comfortable, I think that I'll close my eyes just for a minute or two."

"Where are we now? So, this is what 'home' is! Who are these other two little people and why are they making such a fuss over me? Mother, I don't like it—make them stop coming so close to me, they're scaring me! There's a strange smell in the house, I will later discover that this is what cooked food smells like, but for now, I'm not quite sure how I feel about the smell. I do know that there's a smell that you're not going to be all that happy about—my diaper needs to be changed. It needs to be changed NOW! I don't like how it makes me feel right now."

"My room has beautiful, muted tones that make me feel relaxed. When the shutters and blinds are closed, there's a real cozy ambiance to the room that makes me feel secure. The crib is cozy, and I will soon learn that the things on the mobile hanging above my head are moons and stars and sheep jumping over them. The song that the mobile plays when it's wound up is also quite calming, as long as it's not replayed too often. The favorite part of my room is the antique rocking chair that Mother sits in to nurse me. She will talk to me in her quiet, soothing voice, reassuring me that everything is going to be fine in the world."

"I have to believe her; I feel completely safe with her and Father. They have already set some ground rules for my brother and sister to follow when it comes to me. I wonder why that is exactly. Why do I get so startled whenever they sneak up on me? I really don't like it and let out a loud yell in disapproval until Mother comes and sorts the problem out. Mother and Father seem to be a little more serious with me than they are with the other two children. What's happening in our home that I need to be aware of? I just want to be normal and be treated just like everybody else. This is quite difficult to do though because one of the doctors at the hospital mentioned to Mother and Father that I may be a Highly Sensitive Child."

"What does that even mean? I know that I was showing some sensitivities to the tags in my clothes. Could this be it?"

"Could it be that I can't deal with lots of people being around me all the time?"

"Could it be that I feel safe with my parents, but not so much with anyone else?"

"They keep saying Kelly to me, could that be my name? I certainly hope so, it sounds pretty."

"I love looking around to see the different things in my room, especially when Mother is there and takes the time to show me some of my soft toys. When she puts them against my hands or face, some of the textures feel funny. She's beginning to notice that I have an inquisitive nature and that I need to be sure of certain people before I'm comfortable going to them. I can see her watching me, trying to figure out what I'm thinking. Does she even realize that I can see, hear, and feel everything that's going on around me at a very deep level?"

"I don't think that I'm the same as these other little people running around the home. They peek in from time to time, but Mother gently shoos them away. She's been doing some research on something called "Highly Sensitive Children." Could this be what's wrong with me? Am I broken? How can I be fixed? Will this mean that Mother and Father will love me less, and the other children more?"

"I'm hungry again! But before I get fed, I really need my diaper changed... Mother! Where are you? I really need you!"

"Oh Mother, why do you look so tired? Why do you look so unhappy? Are those tears in your eyes? Is it something that I've done? I hate seeing you so unhappy. I'm going to join you and we can have a good old cry together again."

A Mother's Love

From the moment our tiny daughter was born, we noticed immediately that she was quite different from our other two children who were now three and six years old, respectively. They had been what you might call 'easy' babies. Not only were their births less stressful, but they seemed to be a lot calmer than baby Kelly has been. From the moment she took her first breath, it sounded like there was something different about her. She was much more vocal than my other children had been. She scrunched her eyes tightly trying to block out the harsh light in the delivery room. She was not happy with being passed from the doctor to the nurse, having to be weighed and measured and only then, being wrapped and handed to my husband who was waiting patiently for our brand-new bundle of joy.

There was definitely something quite unique about this little girly that we hadn't experienced with our other two toddlers and I insisted that the doctor perform a thorough investigation before we left the hospital. The pediatrician stepped in and offered a diagnosis almost immediately. It turned out that Kelly was what was quite commonly referred to as a Highly Sensitive Child. Say what now? I had never heard of the term and neither had my husband. What did this mean for us trying to raise her as parents, and what could we expect from her?

Part of the information provided to us as parents by her pediatrician were lists of many reference books, websites, podcasts, and blogs, where we could gather information about this fairly common personality trait. The doctor made it quite clear that it was neither a disease nor something that could be turned on or off. It was something that she was born with and she belonged to a very select group of 15% to 20% of the world's population who were diagnosed as Highly Sensitive Persons. The correct medical term for it was actually "Sensory Processing Sensitivity" and we were told that this was a character trait that only certain individuals were born with. It was not learned and could therefore not be unlearned. It could definitely be influenced by the environment, which meant that my husband, Patrick, and I would always need to be on the lookout to ensure that Kelly was kept as stress-free as possible.

The pediatrician's words were only beginning to sink in. What did this mean for us as parents? How did we need to adapt our lives to a child like this? Was it even possible for Kelly to have a normal life? What did we need to look out for? Were there warning signs if things were about to go upside down?

I was already so exhausted. This had not been the easiest of pregnancies for me and now I understood why. I was probably feeding off of my highly sensitive baby in utero. She was here now though and although she really was a beautiful baby, there were already differences that Patrick and I were able to sense. She was sensitive to certain fabrics and would wiggle and squeal until she was changed. We soon realized that we would need to remove all sizing tags from anything that was going to be against her skin as these chafed her and clearly made her miserable. For the first few days, Kelly cried A LOT!

She didn't like it when too many people were around—not even nurses and doctors. She clearly had issues with Jake and Rebecca (her older siblings). It was explained by the doctor that she would easily become overstimulated and would then need to be calmed down again. He confirmed that it should be up to both Patrick and I to assume this responsibility because there were going to be days when I was just too tired to cope on my own.

I had never heard of this character trait and initially thought that the pediatrician was having us on. After all, by baby number three, I was kind of a seasoned mom, and definitely didn't need some young pediatrician telling me that this is how my newborn was going to behave. Boy, I was so wrong. Even in the hospital, Kelly cried about everything. If she was startled suddenly by a loud noise, she cried. If the water we used to bathe her was too warm, she cried. If we didn't dress her quickly enough after bathing, she cried. She sure let us know when she was hungry and she only slept by taking short naps.

Naturally, the short naps are what got to me the most because it meant that my body wasn't able to recover quickly enough. I was constantly tired, which made me a little cranky. As the doctor had advised, Kelly would pick up on any and all of our emotions and amplify them right back at us. When I was feeling a bit of the baby blues on day three and Kelly had to undergo some ultraviolet light treatment for jaundice, it meant that I could catch up on some of the sleep I was desperately missing out on. My heart went out to her as she was in the incubator and her tiny hand grasped one of my fingers tightly. At least she knew that I was there, and her anxiety seemed to subside slightly.

She could sense my moods, however, and whenever I was feeling even slightly down, Kelly responded in a similar way. Being able to head home was a tremendous blessing because I knew that Patrick and I would be able to navigate this journey together. Maternity clinics are only able to offer so much and it would be great to try and settle into some sort of routine. Kelly was unsure of the car seat and it was immediately clear that she hated the stark contrast of bright outdoor sunlight versus the slightly dimmed lighting inside of the maternity center. She made it quite clear to us what she wanted by exercising her three-day-old lungs at full volume. She had similar reactions to strange smells, loud noises, whenever she needed her diaper changed, or if she was hungry. There would be no getting away from this demanding little creature.

Once at home, Jake and Rebecca would often want to go and play with her or help out by fetching things to make my life easier.

Kelly was very clear on who she wanted near her and who needed to maintain their distance. She was extremely observant, and it was as though she was taking everything in around her that she could possibly see. She loved it when I would nurse her and rock her to sleep on my grandmother's rocking chair beside her crib. Putting her back in her crib was another story altogether though. She very clearly enjoyed being held and soothed by me—Patrick came a close second, although obviously he wasn't able to nurse her!

It wasn't too long before Kelly had the entire household routine falling in with her own. This meant that whenever Kelly went down for her nap, everyone else needed to take a nap as well. The house needed to be quiet enough so that Kelly could sleep soundly. Even the slightest distraction meant that she was awake, and her routine was disrupted. This always ended in tears—mainly hers, but I must admit that there were many days when I was on the verge of a nervous breakdown, only to drag myself back from the cliff-face so that my emotions wouldn't be taken on by Kelly.

Patrick's Perspective

Patrick and Kirsten had been high school sweethearts, dated through college, got married and settled into family life only once Patrick had a stable job. He was the most thoughtful and caring man Kirsten could ever have asked for. As a father, Patrick doted on Jake and Rebecca and Kirsten just knew it would be the same with Kelly. Always being present for the birth of his children, Patrick was surprised when Kelly was screaming her lungs out as she was being passed from the doctor to one of the nurses. At least she had a healthy set of lungs on her! She had screamed much more than Jake or Rebecca had, and Patrick just put it down to complications Kirsten had with her pregnancy.

Could it be that this whole time, Kelly had been feeding off of Kirsten's emotions and anxiety? Was that the reason that Kelly was classified as a Highly Sensitive Child? The more that Patrick began to research the topic of Highly Sensitive Children, the more he realized that Kirsten had probably been sensing Kelly's highly-charged emotional state while she was pregnant. This is what had led to her high anxiety levels, her tearful couple of months, not to mention all of the mood swings that were totally out of sync with Kirsten's normal emotional demeanor.

Now that Kelly was here, they were going to need to be the strongest possible tag team husband and wife couple possible to provide emotional stability for Kelly, because it was only going to get tougher for her out in the big, wide world, the older Kelly got. Patrick realized that this was a lifetime commitment and not just something that they had to do for the first couple of months of Kelly's life. Jake had been a colicky baby and Patrick remembered having to take care of him from time to time to allow Kirsten to get some much-needed rest. This was very different though, because the commitment was likely going to be for most of their lives (or at least until Kelly was able to stand up for herself).

Patrick had read that, as babies, these children could be extremely demanding, but they could also be an absolute pleasure if handled correctly. Both Patrick and Kirsten would need to come up with a child-rearing strategy that would benefit Kelly, while not alienating Jake and Rebecca. The family unit needed to be preserved for all concerned.

Right now though, all that Patrick was really concerned about was getting Kelly and Kirsten settled into some form of routine that would work for Kirsten. From everything he'd read, the very first step would be helping Kirsten to be as stress-free as possible. Even working through the baby blues with her would allow her important time to be able to bond with the newest addition to the family. He helped when it came to bathing and changing Kelly, each time ensuring that he remained calm and gentle with her, just as the books and blogs had suggested.

He realized that, as Kelly was becoming accustomed to her environment, she was also settling into a routine. Kirsten and Patrick kept the shutters and curtains drawn most of the time so that the light in her room was ambi-

The Highly Sensitive Person

ent rather than harsh sunlight. As they introduced Jake and Rebecca to Kelly, and they explained that Kelly reacted to loud noises, bright lights, and other forms of stimulation more than they did, so she needed to be treated differently.

Jake and Rebecca nodded as though they were taking it all in, but Patrick knew that it was going to take quite a bit of time, effort, and energy on everyone's part to get their little family perfectly synchronized so that Kelly's needs could come first. Between Kirsten and himself, they would have to put a plan in motion where the family dynamic was altered. Naturally, Jake and Rebecca were very important parts of that dynamic. Patrick and Kirsten just needed to come up with an action plan for the rest of their lives.

CHAPTER 3:
HIGH SENSITIVITY IN AN INSENSITIVE WORLD

"How do you ever explain the feelings of anxiety and paralyzing fear? I can't answer those questions. It's just a feeling of 'Am I crazy? Am I too sensitive to be in this world?' A feeling that the world is just too complicated for me right now, and I don't feel like I belong here. But it passes, and fortunately today I feel blessed for all the good things in my life."
~ *Winona Ryder*

People incorrectly assume that Highly Sensitive Persons are introverts, while non-sensitive people are extroverts. Using these two labels to distinguish one from the other can be a mistake. Of all HSPs, around 30% are actually extroverts and can thrive under the spotlight as well as any non-sensitive person. They even enjoy being around other people. These terms are not good enough to use as a measuring stick for HSPs. They've been labeled with many names that actually make them feel even worse about themselves internally than they do already. Other children can also tell that they're different because they're more hesitant to get involved immediately. They may even come across as being shy, or judgmental with other children when, in reality, they're processing their feelings deeply.

Usually from a young school-going age, the Highly Sensitive Child would have been labeled by their peers, their classmates and sadly, even by some teachers, because they happened to be different from the rest of the children. Their first day of school may have been spent on the sidelines, quietly observing everything happening around them. They would have identified who the kind kids were that should have been okay to play with and those to avoid. They may have even spotted another one or two other Highly Sensitive Children. These would definitely be good to have as allies and as part of the support structure in school.

The best situation would be for a Highly Sensitive Child to have others understand where they're coming from. They need to be able to take a break whenever they start feeling overwhelmed or overstimulated. One of these classes would be "music time" where each child would get to pick out musical "instruments" to bang and clatter around during that part of the school day. This was likely to cause sensory overload with a Highly Sensitive Child and they may have been seen cowering away, hiding their faces, or covering their ears to block out some of the noise. If you are the adult and you have to deal with this scenario, it will be worth your while to get some good quality headphones where simple, peaceful music could be played for these children instead. This will not only calm them during music time, but you will notice that they will come out of this lesson more relaxed than previously.

This activity would act as a mini-self-care rejuvenation method—the act of having a "time-out" just for themselves while everyone else attempts their hand at making music with pieces of wood, xylophones, castanets, music recorders, metal triangles, and other basic musical instruments. While all this background clatter is going on, the Highly Sensitive Child is able to calm their overloaded mind and restore their balance for the remainder of the day. It may be worthwhile separating the Highly Sensitive Child(ren) from the non-sensitive children, allowing them a quiet space to listen to and process the gentle music. When teachers understand the differences between HSPs and non-HSPs, they would become more proficient at working toward a common goal alongside the parents of these children. Instead of trying to force HSPs to conform to a set of standards alongside the rest of the students, as a teacher, be open to shifting a few things around to accommodate the HSP student(s).

Generally speaking, if a Highly Sensitive Child is being raised in a loving, supportive environment, then they have probably been given some coping mechanisms to ignore all of the taunting from other voices in the world. Some HSPs, when in the right environment, can flourish and bloom just like the beautiful orchids they are—yet, with the same tenacity as that of a dandelion. Whether HSPs survive and thrive is determined by their environment. It depends on how supported they are in all environments. Given the right set of circumstances, they are capable of experiencing peace and happiness (Sand, 2016 – Highly Sensitive People in an Insensitive World).

You may be a Highly Sensitive Person and already know that you are acutely aware of the world around you and everything that's going on around you. Do you realize the way you see and feel about things around you is not the same as everyone else's? You'd be forgiven if you expected others to be exactly the same as you are. After all, we all share common physical characteristics such as eyes, hair, eyes, nose, body parts, etc. Who knew that there would be such a difference regarding internal responses to external stimuli? Where a normal individual would experience things happening around them, sum up their surroundings, and normally jump right in, there's quite a big difference for an HSP. Their system practically overloads with information as they try and process everything for themselves on a much deeper level.

According to Elaine Aron, founder of the term HSP, who has devoted most of her life as a research psychologist to working with Highly Sensitive Persons and Highly Sensitive Children, the HSC usually displays the following strengths or limitations in a classroom environment:

- Accepts the need to plan ahead regarding deadlines.
- Is attentive and vigilant.
- Dislikes being the center of attention unless ready and recognized for their efforts.

- Doesn't function well under the pressure of timed assessments.
- Is excellent at being creative.
- Holds off when disapproval is given.
- Is inquisitive.
- Is easily humiliated.
- Is meticulous in their work.
- Needs to be praised whenever they achieve something.
- Picks up on instructions easily.
- Seldom needs to be disciplined.
- Is a self-starter.
- Is thoughtful.

When your HSC starts school, everything is going to overwhelm them at first and they will feel overstimulated most of the time. Some of the challenges they face have to do with adjusting to the new environment. Aron refers to Highly Sensitive Persons as needing time to "reflect and recover." The start of a new school year is a time when the Highly Sensitive Person needs to be able to socialize and make new friends. Parents of an HSP should prepare them for the transition they will be going through because their period of being able to reflect and recover is going to be a lot shorter than normal.

One of the most important steps when starting school is being able to adjust to making bonds with others socially. Trying to balance forming these new relationships together with taking sufficient time to recharge from overstimulation can be difficult. Most HSPs find the beginning of a new school year to be extremely challenging. This can be short-circuited if things are explained to them and they know exactly what to expect.

Developing close bonds with others on the first day of every school year is something that's important for a Highly Sensitive Person to get right. This will prevent them from feeling left out at a later stage or being given one of the many labels that HSPs are often given because they are so different from non-sensitive people. Parents of Highly Sensitive Children should explain to them some of the demands that will be placed on them before it happens. This helps the transition to be less traumatic for them. Parents also hold the key to preventing many labels being given to their child, simply by explaining the needs of an HSC to the teacher.

If the teacher is aware that the child is not playing up during "music time" because they want to be difficult, they can be more accommodating to meet the Highly Sensitive Child's specific needs. Parents can provide possible solutions for teachers based on how the child is treated at home, rather than frustrating the teacher, or allowing the teacher to become irritated by the HSC. Within the home environment, the HSC may have quite a degree of structure that they are used to, giving them enough "downtime" for them to relax and unwind from being highly stimulated or overwhelmed.

For the HSC returning to school at the beginning of a new school year may find transitioning with new students or new teachers challenging. It would be wise for parents not to overschedule their HSC so their complete focus can be placed on dealing with the stress of the new school year. Parents and teachers should watch that the Highly Sensitive Child is not becoming overanxious, depressed, or listening to their biggest nemesis, their inner critic.

Some ways to deal with this is by remaining firmly grounded in the present and taking the best self-care measures possible. Some of best ways to take care of themselves according to Nikki Anderson, a Highly Sensitive Person includes (Andersen, 2018):

Animal Therapy

Spend some time with your pet. There's something to be said from stroking your cat, hugging your dog, saddling up your horse or being mesmerized by your goldfish for a while. Just being part of nature and close up to those within your home have therapeutic effects. Cats are said to absorb negative energy, although I personally believe that they give off positive vibrations when purring. Many cats are able to sense if there is something wrong and will often come directly to you. Dogs often know just what we need and will place themselves close to where you are, as a means of being close by.

There's a reason why horses are used for equine therapy. According to Dr. Constance Scharff, working with horses constantly through grooming and caring for them relieves us of stress, and creates a sense of overall well-being. They mirror our emotions which can be beneficial for a Highly Sensitive Person to identify that they are overwhelmed and need to take a breath to calm down.

Avoid Negativity and Toxicity

There is a problem when it comes to wanting to please everyone to avoid negativity. You don't want to earn the title of being a People Pleaser or have to deal with individuals who are going to do their best to put you down. Try and steer clear of these individuals as much as possible and remember not to beat yourself up whenever you've made a mistake. We all make them, yet it is time to own our mistakes, look for lessons that we can learn from them, and then move on from there. If people are the cause of us feeling inferior, we should recognize this and cut ties with them as a matter of urgency.

Benefits of Breathing

Breathing can be beneficial, especially when you focus on filling your lungs to capacity, breathing in through your nose, and exhaling out of your mouth. Breathing can be a form of meditation, so focus on inhaling.

Benefits of Soaking

There's something deeply therapeutic of taking a long, hot bath that's been filled with bath crystals or essential oils. Instead of soaking with harsh light overhead, find as many candles as you can and tone down the light in the bathroom. The fragrances will fill your senses and the candlelight will help to restore your emotions to where they need to be.

Cheat with Chocolate
Chocolate contains antioxidants which trigger your happy hormones. It's important that you can learn to snack on these without feeling guilty. Opt for the darkest chocolate available to get the greatest benefit from the antioxidants.

Date for One
Set regular dates for yourself in your diary. These don't need to be expensive or extravagant events. They can be as simple as taking yourself to a local café for a mocha java or visiting a local museum or art gallery. If you're not sure where to start, look on your local tourism websites for places that are within your neighborhood. The most important rule when it comes to these dates is being able to keep them. These will give you some of the "alone" time that you often need as a Highly Sensitive Person.

Discard Clutter
Clutter and leaving areas untidy or overcrowded can provide visual overload for someone who is a Highly Sensitive Person. Consider what your room looks like

from the moment you walk into the space. What can be ditched, donated, given away, sold, or packed away? When working through this process, it's important that you're as ruthless as possible so that you don't end up having to repeat the process on a regular basis.

Find the Support of other HSPs

The only people who will truly "get" where you are coming from are other Highly Sensitive Persons. You both have a unique way of viewing the world. Connecting with a kindred spirit will help you to cope when you're feeling overstimulated.

Get Creative

Tap into your creative side. This advice is relevant whether you've ever done anything creative before or not, even if it's a form of doodling. Spend some time being creative. Some ideas include working on a canvas and simply splashing paint across it. Other ideas might include scrapbooking, writing poetry, woodwork, and others. Let your creative side loose and allow it to float freely.

Get Fit

Find ways to exercise, even if it's walking the dog for 30 minutes a day. Cardio and aerobics exercise are best. Find exercises that you enjoy, however, otherwise you won't stick with them. One of the most important components when it comes to getting fit is having the tenacity to see it through. Whether it's swimming, horse riding, dancing, or hiking in the areas surrounding your home, choose exercises that appeal to your senses.

Grab a Good Book

Get lost in the pages of a good book. It can act as a means of distraction from the harsh reality of life even if only for a short while. This can provide the perfect escape mechanism for you.

Identify Your Values

This is one of the most important aspects that you can address as a means of self-care. By being able to identify what's most important to you, you can truly begin to become your true, authentic self. There are certain areas that you may have identified as representing strong values. What is important, however, is that you treat yourself with kindness, patience, and forgiveness. Although this will take a lot of effort, it will be worth it in the long run.

Magic of Music

Music has the magical power of calming our emotions, especially when the music is uplifting. Create special playlists to match your moods and that way, whenever you feel yourself slipping into an emotional mood, you can stop yourself by putting your headphones on to keep control. Music has been used for emotional healing and well-being for centuries. We are fortunate today that we get to simply plug headphones into our phones and we're all set to be transported to happier times or listen to the soothing sounds of music that mean something to us.

Paying Attention to Emotions

If you can feel your emotions changing during the day, then it's important to try and catch them before they run away with you. As a Highly Sensitive Person, one of the things you should be paying attention to is beginning to feel overwhelmed. The moment you feel this anxiety building, make a point of taking a breather to center and find your calm space. Something as simple as taking a short brisk walk can reduce the stress of a busy office.

Pen to Paper

Discover the therapeutic art of freeform writing. This could be one of the ways you use to cope. Being able to process events, trauma, emotions, and negative experiences can help you put the past behind you. It is also one way to benchmark progress that you may have made over a specific timeframe. Writing allows you to express yourself freely where there is no one who is sitting in judgment of you. One of the most important things about journaling and writing is that it should be kept confidential and not shared with anyone. It's only through this process, that writing can be an effective therapeutic tool.

Resting Enough

It's important that you get enough sleep, in order to function properly. A highly-strung person requires more sleep than most. It's not recommended that you go for more than two nights without a full eight hours of sleep per night. One of the main reasons for this as a Highly Sensitive Person is that you're prone to emotional burnout. Your mind doesn't work the same way as non-sensitive people. Your brain is permanently in overdrive because of your nervous system. It's only through sleep that your system can recharge and rejuvenate itself.

Say Hi to Herbal

Rather than drinking caffeinated drinks at night, switch to herbal teas that can have therapeutic properties. Drinking tea before retiring for the night is much better for your health than anything else. Try different variations until you find just the right blend. Certain blends, such jasmine blossoms, rose petals, lavender, and lemon balm can help with relaxation, as can chamomile.

Unplug

Say "cheers" to social media for a while. This doesn't need to be forever, but realize that this is a distraction and can be the cause of overstimulation. It can also introduce you to feel as though you need to compete with others all the time, and that your life is constantly under a microscope. Constantly having a steady stream of messages from other people's lives can make you feel as though you're coming up short. Detoxing from social media for a while can be a good thing.

Vacation

Set aside some time to travel, even if it's locally. Seeing different landscapes and scenery can shift your energy. Even getting away on a road trip can brighten and lighten your mood. For some though, the mere thought of travel could prove overwhelming.

External Overload

Because Highly Sensitive Persons tend to process things so deeply, and because everything is absorbed, sensory, and mental overload happens much quicker than with a non-HSP individual. The reason for this is due to the processes taking place in the brain. The brain is divided into two specific systems when it comes to processing data. The first of these is the rational brain which is used for cognition and understanding. The second, the limbic brain, deals with emotions and irrational thoughts. When your limbic brain is stimulated, the cognitive brain shuts down and goes to sleep. This heightens your emotional brain, and it believes that your system is now in real danger. This leads to emotions of high stress and anxiety. Because of the feelings of higher stress and anxiety, your "fight-freeze-or-flight" response is triggered and sent into high gear. According to Julie Bjelland, "Most HSPs spend more time in the emotional brain than non-HSPs" (Bjelland, 2018).

Given certain life experiences, the above emotional rollercoaster is likely to happen more and more frequently. Things like speaking in front of a group of people, having to deliver a presentation in a room full of strangers, applying for a new job, or even simple life experiences such as attending social functions can send you over the edge.

Knowing what the cause of the stressor or the trigger is can sometimes help you to feel better because you can internalize this and deal with it. Other times, triggers are not as easy to spot and you may need to dig deeper to discover what's causing your brain to feel completely overwhelmed.

For HSPs, the limbic system in the brain is consistently overactive and needs to be brought under control. The good news is that this can happen with some simple exercises, rather than having to go through a highly emotional or volatile state.

Julie Bjelland works with HSPs all over the world, especially when they are in states of emotional overload. Discovering the difference between what's real and what's not is one way to deal effectively with interpretations that the brain is making.

Recognize Emotional Irritants

Here's how to identify emotional irritations as soon as they occur. This could be anything from your pulse beginning to race, your heart beating faster than normal, or feelings of anxiety rising. Bjelland suggests taking a pen and paper and actually writing down everything that's happened to cause you to feel this way. Possibly, you are in the company of someone, you're in a certain place, or you're at a specific event. By learning to bypass or avoid the reactionary part of the brain and finding another neural pathway, you can retrain the brain to prevent it from again becoming activated by the event or individual. To get this right, there are three steps you need to take:

Pay attention to discover what is setting you off. This is important because not all irritants are obvious. Some occur so subtly that they go unnoticed until it's too late and you're already in the middle of a situation, finding yourself overstimulated and overloaded.

The next step would be to realize that you can either go down the normal slippery slope to becoming emotionally overloaded or you can forge a brand-new neural pathway for yourself. The most important thing of all is being able to recognize that you are in an undesirable state.

She refers to the resultant state as being able to "pause and reflect." This would occur before a conventional melt-down. At this point, you would have a choice as to which route you are going to choose. Nobody is forcing you to head down toward the limbic system. Instead, you will be able to use one or a multitude of the self-care options mentioned above.

External stimuli can come from various sources. This could be anything from police or ambulance sirens to bright flashing lights. Some HSPs describe the sensations that these external stimuli typically have on their senses as being similar to those experienced when someone scratches their nails on a chalkboard. While this sound usually sets the hair on the back of most people's necks on end, it is particularly annoying for an HSP. The same can be said for sudden loud noises, loud music, and large crowds. They need to break away for some quiet time if they are constantly exposed to sensory overload. This is especially true if the Highly Sensitive Person is a teacher, a guest speaker, or has regular contact with large groups of people. In many instances, they explain this to their audience and it's usually not only accepted, but also supported. The HSP is constantly trying to calm external noise factors and strong smells can also overpower them. Everything seems to attack their senses.

Internal Peace and Calm

Highly sensitive people like to "escape" into the world within. As deep thinkers, easily overwhelmed by external influences, having somewhere to escape to as a refuge for them is crucial. For non-sensitive people, they battle to entertain themselves or spend alone time without feeling exactly that—alone! This is where Highly Sensitive Persons are completely different. From the time they are born, they need to have a certain amount of time that is just theirs where they can simply break free from all the chaos and hustle and bustle that is normally experienced by non-sensitive individuals. HSPs all have excellent imaginations, are creative, and find that during this peace and quiet time, they are able to think.

This is where they need to be, even just for a few moments, to shut out all the busyness of the world around them. Unfortunately, the world can also be cruel at times and because of this need for Highly Sensitive Person to be on their own, they can once again be labeled as being anti-social, introverts, freaks, or just plain too soft. This can be challenging for males who are highly sensitive because society demands the typical role of all men to be extremely masculine and tough, rather than having a sensitive side (which is typical of HSPs). The world wants men to be tough rather than having ones who shy away from violent movies or other gruesome scenes that have become a part of our everyday life in the 21st century.

Author of *The Highly Sensitive Person's Survival Guide: Essential Skills for Living Well in an Overstimulating World*, Ted Zeff, explains that often, these labels leave males feeling guilt and shame as a boy because he wasn't as aggressive and tough as his non-sensitive peers (Zeff, 2004).

Chapter 4:
The Highly Sensitive Person's Gifts to the World

"The real warriors in this world are the ones that see the details of another's soul ... They see the transparency behind walls people put up. They stand on the battlefield of life and expose their hearts transparency, so others can finish the day with hope. They are sensitive souls that understand that before they could be a light, they first had to feel the burn."
~ Shannon L. Alder

No matter whether you are a Highly Sensitive Person or a non-sensitive person, we each possess strengths and limitations that have a profound impact on the way we interact with the world. Understanding how some of the gifts might be used to beautify the world around you and uplift the lives of others could make a difference to how you view being a Highly Sensitive Person. Many highly sensitive individuals just wish that they could shut things off for a while, and become normal, or as normal as the rest of the world. The truth is that the world desperately needs those who are highly sensitive as well.

Imagine a world where there was no empathy or compassion and no appreciation for the finer things in life such as the arts or music. These are all areas that Highly Sensitive Persons would be drawn to because they bring out the best in them. They feel safe and secure in being able to freely create or design things. These are ways for them to express themselves, especially in a world that can be harsh and insensitive. Before discussing some of the many talents and skills that HSPs bring to the world, Dr. Elaine Aron describes the way that HSPs feel about everything around them by using a simple acronym; D.O.E.S.

Although this only covers a few points about Highly Sensitive Persons, it captures some of the more important characteristics. According to this acronym, "D" describes the depth of processing information that a Highly Sensitive Person will experience. Subconsciously, we are constantly processing information. We read signs and interpret their meanings, we look for cues in peoples' faces and in their body language, we listen to language being used, and we look for meaning in our surroundings. We know that if it's raining, we're likely to get wet, unless we do something about it, so we pack in an umbrella to avoid it.

For the HSP, this "depth of processing" happens on a level where the analysis of situations is very deep. They search for patterns and symbolism in things that non-sensitives take for granted and accept as-is.

Next, comes the "O" for Overstimulation. We know that HSPs have a limit to how much stimulation they can take before they begin to feel completely overwhelmed by everything. For school- and college-going HSPs, this could occur on a normal day where they return home and need time out to recharge completely. Overstimulation can also occur from attending large social gatherings, or visiting large shopping centers, or overcrowded stores. Anywhere that there's too much happening, too many bright lights, and loud music could lead to overstimulation. Once again, the Highly Sensitive Person needs to retreat to safety in order to return to a natural state of peace and stability before attending to another busy schedule.

As parents of an HSP, it's important that the child is not overwhelmed by extracurricular activities. They should be presented with opportunities to do things that they're interested in, but they will probably fare much better at activities that only include a tutor and themself. Some examples of this could be piano lessons, art lessons (where it's just the teacher and them), any sport that is one-on-one—horse riding may be an excellent way for them to spend time connecting with a horse—and spending quiet time alone in nature. This could be an excellent way for a Highly Sensitive Person to destress.

Becoming overwhelmed occurs more often and faster with HSPs than with non-sensitive individuals. Try to limit those activities that are likely to stress the Highly Sensitive Person out. This could be anything from attending a house party to a busy rock festival with loud music, bright lights, and large groups of people.

Both sides of the emotional spectrum are represented in the "E" for Emotional Reactivity. For an HSP, the highs they experience are many more than non-HSPs will experience exactly when enduring the same activity. Emotional highs are much higher, verging on euphoria, while their lows are devastating low. When they experience conflict with someone, they can feel such emotional pain and sadness that it feels that their entire world is coming to an end. "E" also represents empathy.

Their empathy is not as the world would have us define empathy. Instead, they take on all the emotions of everyone around them. This is more than merely feeling conventional empathy and compassion for those around them. Instead, they physically take on the actual feelings of others, according to Dr. Aron. The danger of this is that their emotions can be in a constant state of flux, from extreme highs to extreme lows. Non-sensitive people only have to worry about the emotions that they're feeling, while for HSPs, they not only worry about their own, but they actually absorb the feelings of those around them as though they were sponges.

The final letter in the D.O.E.S. anagram stands for "Sensing the Subtle." This can be exhausting because the HSP picks up on different degrees of differences or shifts in mood. They are quick to notice strange smells, and fragrant scents that are in the night air that those around them miss completely. Where this becomes a negative is when they can sense a shift in mood or when others are trying to keep a "stiff upper lip," due to tension in a relationship—the HSP is able to not only sense this, but they physically take each of these emotions on.

Some of the many gifts that HSPs bring to the world are as follows (E. Aron, 2020):

Strengths

Visual perception: They are open to seeing a great many things that others miss. They also see things with such clarity that they are able to recall this information in high-definition detail as if the images were directly in front of them. This makes them excellent at paying high attention to detail. Any employment that needs someone to be 100% conscientious of high-quality output is where Highly Sensitive Persons shine.

They are excellent friends, colleagues, partners, and roommates because of their attentive nature. They pay particular attention toward making those around them happy, because it makes them feel happy in return.

Because they think deeply, they can hold interesting conversations with others because they do more than just skim over the surface. HSPs can fully immerse themselves in various topics of conversation, making them interesting conversationalists.

They get on with others mainly because they understand their emotions.

Because they are so good at processing information, they can pick things up much quicker without having to study as much because they're processing constantly.

Because they're so conscientious and able to focus so intently on a task at hand, they are excellent when it comes to processing tasks that require fine motor skills.

They are highly creative when it comes to problem-solving and thinking in general.

Highly Sensitive Persons have strong intuition and they usually rely on this to make important decisions.

HSPs are sensitive to nuances in meaning. If those around them are speaking with certain intonations, highly sensitive individuals are ideal at picking up on these nuances and interpreting them accurately.

They are emotionally aware which leads to greater understanding of people, situations, and possibly even tensions that are undercurrents that others may not pick up on.

Creativity: Because Highly Sensitive Persons prefer spending time alone, they are often extremely creative, as this provides them with a way to release their tension and cope with their emotions.

Just as Highly Sensitive Persons have many strengths and gifts to share with the world, they also have several weaknesses which are listed below:

Limitations

Overstimulation: they can become hyper-stimulated by their surroundings as well as by individuals, they are often overwhelmed by situations and need to escape to recover.

They take on the emotions of others. While this could be a strength, it can also be a limitation because the HSP doesn't know how to switch this off. They have no way of preventing their system from going into emotional overdrive.

Thrive on alone time: alone can be beneficial to the HSP; however, long stretches of isolation from human contact can be detrimental and can even lead to symptoms of anxiety and depression.

Perfectionism: The need for everything to be perfect can wreak havoc on the Highly Sensitive Person. One of the reasons for this is that they are often inwardly critical of the quality of their work, missing deadlines, and self-berating when it comes to judging themselves.

Different from mainstream society: Their difference from the rest of the world can be seen as a limitation if they are constantly negative and hard on themselves.

In most instances, they will know that they are different from everyone else because they've probably been told that throughout their lives. When they know this already. It deeply wounds and offends them to be told that they're "too sensitive" and need to "lighten up."

All About Abby

I've known Abby my whole life. Because she's a few years younger than I, and we grew up in the same social circles, I knew her from the time she was a young girl. I'm not sure whether it was because she was slightly chubby as a young girl, whether she was extremely shy, or whether it was because she was definitely a Highly Sensitive Person that Abby held back throughout her entire childhood. My guess is that it's the latter, relying on my new understanding about Highly Sensitive Persons. She refused to participate in group or team events, or even culturally. Whenever we were together, and she needed to do a reading or give a speech in front of a crowd, she would completely shy away from the assignment, even if the group was of people whom she knew.

As a teenager, Abby's social life was non-existent. She would bury herself in romance novels, feel-good movies, and baking. Abby loved spending time in the kitchen with her mother and grandmother who were highly skilled when it came to culinary arts. This gave her the creative outlet she needed, apart from being extremely talented and creative with computer graphics and design. She would always decline invitations to parties or dances because she felt that others were mocking her or speaking about her behind her back. None of this was real of course, but for Abby, it felt very real.

Abby is a typical Highly Sensitive Person, although she doesn't know it. Yes, there are still many individuals in society who have never even heard of HSPs. This is not an impossibility as the term had not been invented while

Abby was growing up. During her childhood, insensitive people labeled her with all sorts of unkind names from being a spoilsport, a crybaby, or introverted. If you consider the different characteristics that Dr. Aron used to identify someone who is a Highly Sensitive Person, there are approximately ten different levels of HSPs in the world. This makes perfect sense. If Abby were to take Dr. Aron's online assessment today, she would probably score in the highest percentile possible. There are several characteristics that lead me to identify Abby as being a typical HSP. This is because she's constantly looking inwards at her own faults and failures.

More often than not, she feels that the whole world is against her and sitting in judgment of everything she does. She's really overly sensitive, and you will often find her curled up in bed or on the sofa with a box of Kleenex and a good book. She declines invitations to socialize unless she knows most of the people who are going to be there. Even when she agrees to attend, she usually limits the time she's there—often being the last to arrive and the first to leave. Whenever people speak in low tones, Abby immediately believes they are talking about her, and she feels overly sensitive about this. Although these are mostly assumptions, her friends tend to keep her at arm's length because they know her well enough to understand that she's overly sensitive to the world around her.

For a while, Abby was really happy because she found another Highly Sensitive Person to connect with. After dating for what seemed like forever, they were married and Abby gave birth to a beautiful baby girl, called Samantha. It was immediately apparent that Samantha had inherited both her parents' sensitive sides. From the time she was born, Samantha reacted to a variety of sensory stimuli; things like bright lights, loud noises, and smells, and she even had a reaction to her woolen socks. As far as labels go, Samantha could be classified as a "Sensory Defensive Person."

College professor Sharon Heller identified these specific traits as being common with this type of HSP:

- Can be extremely ticklish.
- Can't be in large crowds of people for very long.
- Cannot eat certain foods because they dislike the texture.
- Don't deal with visual stimuli very well, especially not bright, flashing lights.

- Irritated by textures against their skin, depending on a variety of fabrics. Not applicable to all textures.
- Loud sounds startle them, especially when they are unexpected.
- Strong odors irritate their senses.

As an HSP herself, it became easy for Abby to identify with some of the things that Samantha was experiencing even as a baby. Tragedy struck Abby and Samantha when Abby's husband was fatally wounded in a motor vehicle accident, and Abby devoted all her time to her daughter, further withdrawing from the world. Her close connection with Samantha meant that they would often feed off one another's emotions. Because mother and daughter were so similar, as Samantha grew, they would both rather remain in the safety of their home environment than putting themselves under the stress of dealing with crowds. They would even choose to shop at smaller strip malls as opposed to large shopping centers where there were likely to be more people to set them off.

As an adult, Abby was able to function within smaller organizations where people relied heavily on her. She is excellent in what she does, overseeing health, safety, and quality assurance for a small-to-medium-sized enterprise. Larger organizations involved her needing to become more involved and she simply didn't have the energy to be dealing with all of the attention. Don't get me wrong, she holds down a responsible position at the moment as daily, she takes on everything that the Chief Executive Officer of the business needs done. She's excellent at her job because of her high attention to detail. As an employee, you might say that Abby goes above and beyond the requirements of her job. She is completely loyal and committed to her work. Some may even say too committed at times, especially when the CEO takes advantage of her working after hours, on holidays, and even on some weekends.

Abby makes a great friend, especially if you're looking for someone to always rely on and lend a listening ear, when you're feeling down. She's quick to sense when there's something wrong and on the days when you're feeling down, it's not unusual to receive a brief motivational text from her letting you know that she's thinking about you. She's genuine in the assistance that she offers, although you know that if it's anything to do with crowds, she's likely to refuse. In one-on-one situations, she's perfectly fine. Even with people she knows and feels comfortable, she can still feel things intensely and take on emotions without even realizing it. Because Abby was born long before Dr. Aron coined the term "Highly Sensitive Person," Abby was given no special treatment concerning the way that she was raised. She had to figure it out for herself.

Recognizing that her daughter possessed many of the same characteristics, however, made it easier for Abby to insulate Samantha from many of the harsh realities of the world. Both mother and daughter were often labeled as being "way too sensitive" and I've even heard people recommending that they go on antidepressants to deal with their fluctuating mood swings. Abby and Samantha both desperately need to rely on coping mechanisms to help them overcome the major anxiety and pressure that they feel when dealing with large crowds and the pressures of the world around them.

Whenever I managed to get Abby to join me for a quick cup of coffee and a chat, she would confirm that there were indeed several benefits to being a Highly Sensitive Person that others hadn't even thought of. One of these was being able to share the pleasures of one-on-one, alone time with friends. Few people are able to connect on a genuinely intimate level and nobody does it quite as well as a Highly Sensitive Person. In those moments, she often proved to me exactly how genuine friendship could be. During those special one-on-one moments, we were able to talk about absolutely anything and everything and I could appreciate that I had Abby's undivided attention— a quality that is rare in a bustling world today.

If you asked Abby what she enjoyed doing more than anything, she would probably tell you that some of her favorite times of the day would be sunrise and sunset. The reason for this would be that the world seems quite peaceful at those times of day. There would be less movement on the streets surrounding her and she admitted that this was often when she did most of her thinking. In fact, many of Abby's favorite things carried only a small price tag. For example, she would light scented candles and soak in the tub with a good book. Most of the things that Abby found relaxing and rejuvenating were free. This removed the added pressure of having to keep up with a specific lifestyle and spending unnecessary money in doing so.

Abby is physically sensitive to touch as well. She loves the smell of her little Yorkie's puppy breath and finds her cat particularly comforting. Different fabrics against her skin can either make her feel calm and comfortable, or very uncomfortable. In fact, she can spend hours feeling itchy just at the very thought of wearing something disagreeable. As an HSP, Abby can also find herself feeling emotional. Whether it's a piece of music or a love story, she freely admits to being moved by experiencing artistic endeavors. It's not just movies or music that have this effect, it could be the sight of a newborn that reminds her of her own children or tender memories of her late husband.

Because she's so good at connecting things, Abby is more effective at her job than many others would be. Her brain works differently to those around her. Many others are good at remembering facts and information, while Abby is able to focus on the entire picture. She sees the big things, as well as the small intricacies that most would either forget, or overlook completely. She can be extremely creative when it comes to implementing systems and ways to discover new things.

Some of the simplest things make Abby happy. She is quite content with a handmade card from her son as a birthday or a Christmas gift crafted at school. She can become totally mesmerized by a rainbow after the rain and feel elated for most of the day afterward. It really is the small and simple things that give her life meaning.

Something that Abby really knows that she needs to work on are her feelings of low self-esteem. No matter what she does, how many times she is praised for doing a good job, or recognized for her contribution, Abby still feels like a failure and a fraud. She feels that praise is unnecessary and that she's not worthy of it. No matter how many times you try and reassure her and communicate with her that what she does matters and she's making a valuable contribution toward a project, she will always find something that was wrong and focus on that.

In discussions with others, Abby tends to wear her heart on her sleeve and if she trusts you, she will share her whole life story with you. This is only if she feels that you are someone with whom she can confide. This character trait often gets Abby into trouble because not everyone is well-meaning. Some individuals will even take advantage of her good nature. Her misplaced alliances range from relying on someone to keep a secret to having someone confide in her. HSPs must be careful of too much offloading though because of the tendency to absorb the energy onto themselves.

Her whole life has been spent in a quest of trying to "toughen up" to rid herself of the softer side of her personality. This has never really been Abby's problem though. This is actually one of her greatest assets. While trying to discover what made her so different from many of her peers, Abby came across some of the following descriptions of individuals along the HSP spectrum. She was trying to discover exactly where she fits into this spectrum, and where she and Samantha possibly differ. Many of the following answers came from various studies conducted by professors and other reputable research scientists and psychologists, including Dr. Elaine Arons's in 1996. Abby would search the internet, research studies, and other reference material to find answers. She was trying to discover what made her and Samantha seem so different in a world of individuals who hardly seemed to care about the next person. Here are some of the characteristics she discovered:

Individuals Thriving in a Fantasy World

In the 1980s, Michael Shallis, a British researcher, discovered those who are hypersensitive to the flow of electrical current. Through interviewing hundreds of candidates, his research indicated that most of those sensitive to electricity happened to be women. His studies revealed the following trends with these individuals:

Statistics

- 23% had actually been struck by lightning.
- 69% had experienced a paranormal occurrence.
- Another statistic is that 60% became very ill immediately preceding a thunderstorm, or they could predict that one was imminent.
- 70% of those surveyed were hypersensitive to both loud noises and bright lights.
- Some of this group even had an impact on streetlights.
- Those prone to battling with allergies totaled approximately 70%.
- Imaginational
- Easily stressed.
- Bashful.
- Strong desire to be alone.

- Increased compassion for others.
- Superior memory recall.
- Emotional fluctuations.

Kazimierz Dombrowski discovered that there were several definitive areas that HSPs could be divided into as being "super sensitive." These included:

Psychomotor
Some of the behavior of HSPs is directly linked to the way that impulse controls their behavior. They often exhibit nervous tics or habits as a means of expressing their emotion. Inability to sleep (insomnia) is another common characteristic.

Sensory
Their sensory perception is experienced at a high level. They are more likely to experience allergic reactions to things around them. This includes things that can be touched or can touch them. This might include textures of clothing, fabric, or textures of food. Because they are highly sensitive, they need to be nurtured more than most and often seek pleasure from the things that are located immediately around them.

Orchid Children

Professor Bruce Ellis, a professor at the University of Utah who specializes in evolutionary developmental psychology, has defined these individuals as being as delicate and fragile as orchids are in their environment. If you've ever tried to grow orchids, then you know that they need extra special care and constant nurturing if they are to survive, let alone thrive. Just as each of these beautiful and unique flowers needs a great deal of attention, so too do each of these "orchid children." In response to an article, he states that "most children survive and even thrive in whatever circumstances they encounter, like dandelions. Nurtured with good-quality parenting and programs, orchid children can blossom spectacularly into society's happiest, most productive people. Conversely, given poor parenting and sketchy surroundings, they are at greater risk to end up wrestling with depression, substance abuse, and even jail."

Spiritually Sensitive

Highly Sensitive Persons are normally characterized as being psychic. It's believed that they possess extrasensory perception (ESP), and this is more common in this group of HSPs than in others. Whether these can be labeled as actual events or merely "hunches," here are some of the things that make them different:

- They can experience the moods of others.
- They can often 'know' what's about to happen in the future.
- Many of them claim to see movement out of the corners of their eyes.
- If they happen to make a wrong decision, they will often physically report feeling a "knot in the pit of their stomachs."

Slim Boundary Individuals

During the 1980s, Dr. Ernest Hartmann, from Tufts University, recognized the 'boundaries' theory while conducting studies on individuals who were able to recall their dreams with vivid recollection. They were often able to recall dreams that were possibly disturbing. Common characteristics of each of these individuals included some of the following:

- Becoming exhausted and overwhelmed when facing sensory and emotional input.
- Experiencing pleasure and pain more than with non-sensitive individuals.

- Being prone to disease and allergies.
- As children and young adults, they are likely to experience trauma through sensory stimuli overload that becomes difficult to process. Some of these things include loud noises and bright lights.

Fantasy HSPs

Two American psychologists, Theodore Barber and Sheryl Wilson, stumbled across this characteristic in 1981:

- As much as 4% of the population is said to possess this characteristic. Some of the traits include a vivid imagination, and being able to fantasize about many things, as well as experiencing the paranormal.
- It's thought that many of these people are very religious. Joan of Arc saw images and heard voices, and it is because of this that it was believed that she was potentially a Highly Sensitive Person.

Some other characteristics common to these individuals include:

- As children, they are likely to dream.

- They have fantasy friends.
- Sensations they imagine can be felt as though they were genuine.
- They possess psychic abilities.
- Their sensory perceptions are vivid, bright, and colorful.
- They find it tough to tell the difference between fact and fiction.
- They may experience visions.

It doesn't matter where you fall on the HSP spectrum, if you understand that you have sensitivities that need to be addressed, then working through various emotional intelligence solutions will provide you with the answers you seek. These solutions will serve you in not just the short-term, but for the rest of your life. In the chapters that follow, we'll discover more about what emotional intelligence is and how to effectively apply it to your life.

Chapter 5:

HSPs and Emotional Intelligence

"Highly sensitive people tend to have stronger emotional responses than others. Partly, this is because they notice so many emotional cues that others miss, so they're very 'tuned in' to feelings. But it's also because HSPs process things so deeply. Imagine if you felt every emotion five times longer and five times louder; that's kind of what it's like to be an HSP."

~ Andre Sólo

According to Dr. Elaine Aron, the Highly Sensitive Person (HSP) prefers to pause and reflect, sometimes thinking deeply before coming to a decision. A lot of these feelings and emotions are taken on intuitively and subtly, without needing a lot of explanation. Unfortunately, the workings of this highly intuitive self is not something you can decide to switch on or off at the drop of a hat. Because of this, they are overwhelmed by things that wouldn't irritate someone who's a non-sensitive person. As an HSP, you can become totally overwhelmed by the slightest challenge that comes your way. According to the Merriam-Webster dictionary, *intuition* is defined as: the power or faculty of attaining to direct knowledge or cognition without evident rational thought and inference; immediate apprehension or cognition; and knowledge or conviction gained by intuition, or quick and ready insight (Merriam-Webster, 2020).

While there are these typical characteristics of feeling overwhelmed, not dealing with crowds very well. Although a high percentage of HSPs don't cope with large groups of people around them, 30% are actually extroverted.

Because of many of the characteristics common to HSPs, they make naturally good companions when it comes to emotional intelligence. Some of the reasons for this are rooted in their willingness and ability to devote themselves completely to a relationship. Emotional intelligence is all about being able to connect with others in meaningful ways. Over the last few decades, there have been many studies conducted on the importance of healthy emotional intelligence. Many business organizations believe that emotional intelligence is something that should be used to benefit the businesses operation in meeting its organization goals. The truth is that emotional intelligence is so important that it influences every sphere of life.

Emotional intelligence is all about human interaction, communication, self-management, and relationship management, so it makes logical sense that HSPs should be pretty good at it. Unfortunately, when HSPs are in a bad space, or feel dependent on their partner for constant validation and stroking, then this has the opposite effect of solidifying sound relationships. In these occasions, Highly Sensitive Persons would doubt their abilities to be effective in any sphere of emotional intelligence.

John Mayer, an American psychologist specializing in emotional intelligence and personality psychology at the University of New Hampshire, and Peter Salavoy, American social psychologist and President of Yale University, were the first to discover that there was a difference between emotional intelligence and intellectual quotient or IQ. It wasn't until Daniel Goleman published his book, *Emotional Intelligence* in 1996, that companies and individuals began noticing exactly how different emotional intelligence (EQ) was from IQ, and how this discovery made such an impact on the world. EQ is founded on two foundational principles, but separated further than this. It is defined as having the skills to identify, understand, and control not only your own emotions, but doing exactly the same thing with the emotions of others. Feelings can cause us to perform either negatively or positively, depending on the situation. We need to be able to manage our emotions, especially when facing pressurized situations. The challenge comes in when HSPs are already tuned into their own emotions and the emotions of those around them. Given this tendency, does emotional intelligence overwhelm them even further?

What Makes Emotional Intelligence So Important?

Decades ago, before the invention of the internet and computers, people would work in offices where they would seldom have much interaction with each other. Class distinction and education differentiated between those who worked in offices such as finance, law, and other commercial enterprises and those who worked in factories as laborers. As the internet and computers began to hit the market, through IBM for business, the Apple Lisa, and Macintosh, the rules of business began to change.

Where many personal assistants had been men until that time, women began to enter the workplace during the war, and instead of returning to their homes, they remained employed. In the late 1990s, the World Wide Web entered the scene. Suddenly, there was a need for people to begin communicating across borders and virtually reaching out across the world to each other. There had never been a more crucial time to understand how emotion came into play in business, rather than intelligence.

Would you believe that the first time the words "emotional intelligence" appeared was in 1964? It took another 25 years before it was used in a doctorate dissertation by a graduate student, Wayne Leon Payne. This appeared in his paper of 1985. It wasn't until Salovey and Mayer used it in some of their research work in 1990 that it became more popular. Their research was recognized by the fields in which they were conducting their research. Much of this focused on the difference between abilities and how they were influenced by emotions.

As part of their research, these two professors discovered that when it came to identifying their emotions, some individuals were better at it than others. Not only could they identify their feelings, but they were also better at solving problems when those around them were behaving emotionally. They devised two specific assessments that people could use to assess who was more skillful at emotion identification. Part of the reason why Mayer and Salovey weren't highly recognized for the work they did, was because they were focused on academic research.

Mainline research became more widely recognized, thanks to a New York writer who was also a psychologist. At the time, Daniel Goleman wrote for Popular Psychology. He discovered an article written by Mayer and Salovey. At his request, he was given permission to make use of the term "emotional intelligence" for his upcoming book as long as credit was given to those who had originally coined the phrase.

By the time Goleman published *Emotional Intelligence* in 1995, there was a furor that erupted among those who had been researching the information that was constructed originally as a psychological process. When they coined the term "emotional intelligence," Mayer and Salovey described it as being a "form of social intelligence that involves the ability to monitor one's own and others' feelings and emotions, to discriminate among them, and to use this information to guide one's thinking and action" (Riopel, 2019).

One of the studies that was done involved one of their subject groups watching movies that were disturbing. They determined that those who could withstand the intensity of emotions that the movie had invoked could recover quicker than those who found it upsetting. The ability to identify, understand, and name an emotion was referred to as "emotional clarity." These individuals could adapt to the emotions of others during personal encounters.

Instead of emotional intelligence being something solid that has been defined by the professors that discovered it and remaining static, it's something that continues to be studied and seems to be forever changing as new discoveries are made. There have been many different types of researchers who have added value to EQ over the last decade or so. The original framework proposed by Mayer and Salovey, according to Raz and Zysberg, was defined by the following four points:

- Identification of emotions within yourself and others around you.
- Incorporating different emotions into thought processes.
- Being able to work through complex emotions successfully.
- Controlling your own emotions and working through the emotions of others.

Raz and Zysberg continued on to state that emotional intelligence may be responsible for the following important life outcomes:

- Being able to interact with others socially in a positive way.
- Being content with all that life has to offer and general well-being.
- Excellent physical and mental health.
- Improved academic and work performance (Raz & Zysberg, 2014).

Mayer and Salovey published a paper in 1990 that first described emotional intelligence as a revolutionary new idea where emotions could be regulated in day-to-day life.

Daniel Goleman is often recognized as the founder of modern emotional intelligence, although the term was first coined by Mayer and Salovey almost a decade before Goleman published his first book. It was Goleman's books that made the term famous. Many of the academics involved in multiple studies before Goleman's time weren't all that impressed by the direction, as it was felt that he was taking their initial work on the subject.

Goleman posited that certain skills such as awareness of self, and the ability to motivate oneself, were a product of childhood. It was possible, according to Goleman, that these characteristics could still be learned as an adult. Despite not discovering or coining the phrase emotional intelligence, Goleman's work has since been incorporated into companies, schools, and universities across the globe. Goleman proved that a high intellectual quotient (IQ) was no predictor of success in life. The theory that Goleman promoted further expanded on what Salovey and Mayer had come up with:

- Anticipating the emotions of those around you through empathy and compassion.
- Being able to persevere and motivate yourself to overcome challenges as and when they arise.

- Managing relationships with others effectively by using social skills.
- Regulating your emotions and figuring out how to predict possible outcomes or consequences before choosing to act impulsively. Trying to control your own emotions.
- Understanding the emotions you feel moment to moment by being self-aware. Along with this, comes seeking understanding as well.

Differences Between IQ and EQ

EQ is something that's a part of who you are, according to Goleman. While IQ tests predict your ability to do certain things, they could not predict long-term success in life or actual well-being. This soon led to his 20:80 theory. Only 20% is thanks to intellectual quotient, while the remaining 80% is linked to emotional intelligence. Some of the things that emotional intelligence covers includes:

- Impulse control.
- Motivation of self.
- Perseverance.
- Ability to regulate emotions such as compassion, sense of humor, and hope.

The Highly Sensitive Person

Goleman sees both EQ and IQ as working alongside each other in tandem, rather than working together. This is often seen in the workplace where someone is quite intelligent, yet they're hopeless when it comes to relationships with people. This disparity is the reason behind some of the biggest challenges faced in life and business today.

The bestseller, *Emotional Intelligence 2:0* was written by Dr. Travis Bradberry and Dr. Jean Greaves. For them, emotional intelligence is something that can not only be learned, but improved upon, depending on how you score in each of the following areas:

- Self-awareness.
- Self-management.
- Social awareness.
- Relationship management.

Extensive research has been conducted and reported in *Emotional Intelligence 2:0* by Drs. Bradberry and Greaves. More than half a million people were part of the research that makes up this work. These individuals were from all over the world. In addition to assisting with new skills, there is additional information on (Bradberry & Greaves, 2009):

- Cultural changes and emotional intelligence.
- Discrepancies with gender and emotional intelligence.
- Generation difference and emotional intelligence.
- Shifts in society and emotional intelligence.

Mayer and Salovey Method of Emotional Intelligence

According to Leslie Riopel, professor of psychology at Northwood University and authority in the psychology of mindfulness, when Salovey and Mayer introduced emotional intelligence, it was focused on the following four areas of emotion:

Perception: Non-verbal signals and stimuli. Examples of this could include natural landscapes and art.

Facilitation: How we work with our emotions. Moods, environment, reasoning.

Understanding: You can only really understand emotions if you know what different emotions mean, changing your emotions and even creating new emotions.

Management: The management of emotions, your own as well as those of others.

The most challenging of all is that there are definitely discrepancies regarding the research and application of emotional intelligence. Some researchers are adamant that it's a skill that can be learned and adapted to meet the requirements in your life at any given time, while others claim that it's something you are born with as an innate capability. When you consider Highly Sensitive Persons, the latter construct makes sense. They are born with a built-in super radar for emotions, making them highly emotional individuals.

Kendra Cherry, author and speaker, poses the question as to what life would be like if we weren't able to understand, interpret, or know how to respond appropriately to those around us who were sad, depressed, excited, or able to identify a range of emotions. She also suggests that emotional intelligence can be more important when it comes to predicting success than IQ. In her description of the same four categories, she includes the following based on information by Salovey and Mayer (Salovey & Mayer, 1990). Accurate perception of emotions. Often facial expressions and other non-verbal cues such as body language should be accurately understood and interpreted correctly.

We use emotions to help us to determine suitable reactions. Examples of this might be laughing at the sight of something funny or crying during a sad part of a movie. Each of these situations involves us reasoning with different emotions.

A key ingredient to emotional intelligence is being able to interpret and understand emotions and where they come from. We should be able to discern between when we are the cause of an emotional outburst, and when it stems from somewhere that has nothing to do with us at all.

For Cherry, managing our emotions is the highest level of self-regulation that we can aspire to in emotional intelligence. This means being able to understand, decipher, and respond to emotions in the correct way, not just for our own emotions, but toward the emotions of others as well.

The impact of emotional intelligence can be felt in various aspects of our lives daily. For someone who is advanced in emotional intelligence, they know that emotions can be fleeting, lasting only for a short time before moving onto something different. The individual who is healthy when it comes to their level of EQ knows this and doesn't escalate a delicate situation. Instead, they may wait out the irritation, allowing it to pass before they approach with a comment or question. These situations often occur in the workplace.

Strong, emotionally intelligent individuals are aware of their own feelings as well as the feelings of those around them. They understand that various things contribute toward their emotions. They take all of these factors into consideration.

Having empathy is one of the most important aspects of emotional intelligence. It requires being able to understand how you would act or react if you placed yourself in the individual's immediate situation. Being able to do this is often referred to as having compassion for the next person. You can apply emotional intelligence in diverse ways during each day. Examples of the way this could happen daily include, but aren't limited to (Cherry & Lehman, 2020):

- Accepting criticism and assuming responsibility.
- Accepting others for who they are without passing judgment.

- Being empathetic toward others.
- Being strong enough to say "No" when you need to.
- Moving forward once you've made a mistake, once again assuming responsibility and accountability.
- Really listening to others.
- Sharing how you feel with those around you.
- Solving problems in creative ways that work for everyone.
- Understanding why you do the things you do.

Highly Sensitive People and Emotional Intelligence

According to the co-author of *Emotional Intelligence 2:0*, Travis Bradberry, HSPs are often misjudged and given additional negative labels, all because they interpret emotions completely differently from the other 80% of the population. They are much more perceptive and pick up on the different subtle nuances, facial expressions, body language, and even the mood in a room that non-HSPs would miss. They do more than just hearing the words that someone says. HSPs can become masters of emotional intelligence once they understand and accept that they are actually highly sensitive to begin with.

Once they know that they are HSPs, they can become aware of their own emotions faster and can learn to deal with them more quickly when they are negative. He describes the Highly Sensitive Person from an emotional intelligence perspective as:

Criticism is especially hard to hear and even more difficult to accept from others. Unlike your non-sensitive peers, you take everything to heart and can overreact. Simply shrugging it off and getting over it is something that your highly sensitive mind won't allow you to do. It's this endless rumination about the "could have, would have, should have," that keeps the situation playing over and over again in your mind. Believe it or not, this is actually something that's quite positive. This gives you the opportunity to replay the scenario in your mind until you can come up with a suitable solution.

Being detail-oriented is another benefit for HSPs because they pay as much attention to minute details as they do to the feelings of those around them. Because they are so attentive, you will find that their work is usually extremely detailed. They're the type of individuals who would be sure to dot all their i's and cross all their t's. Depending on the profession they're in, this could be hugely beneficial for a wide range of jobs that require staff who can focus on the details. For these HSPs, picking up errors and inconsistencies is as easy for them as picking up when there's tension in the air.

Highly sensitive people have excellent manners because they pick up on the emotions of those around them. They are people pleasers and can sense how their own mood is influencing the way that others are feeling. They can also sense the moods of others. HSPs have a problem with people who are unnecessarily rude.

They work extremely well as part of a team. They are also well-respected for their input within a team environment. This is mainly because they pay close attention to the feelings of others in the team. The only downside when it comes to being efficient as a team player is if it's necessary for them to make a decision. HSPs are better at providing input, analyzing information sets, and checking that things are done in an orderly fashion. When it comes to the final head's-up, they're not as efficient.

HSPs battle to let mistakes and bad decisions go. These often haunt them for weeks, months, and even years later. Unlike their counterparts, HSPs battle to move past a decision that leads to failure. This often prevents them from moving forward and making new plans and decisions when necessary. This can incite a degree of fear that is very real for the HSP that limits their decision-making process.

Even the thought of working in an open plan office is enough to make an HSP cringe. The close proximity of everyone else, the noise factor, the constant stimuli that's happening all the time is just too much for the Highly Sensitive Person. Even things like odors will negatively affect them and in all likelihood, their level of productivity will be negatively impacted. For these individuals, they require the solitude and silence of their own space and own office. This is where they are able to perform at their optimum.

There's a reason why HSPs are known as being overemotional. They react emotionally to even the slightest stimulus. For them, it's often toward the emotions of others that they react the most. They battle to let these emotions go once they become invested in them. These don't need to be their own emotions. In many instances, they're taking on how someone else is feeling or behaving and they're able to channel each of these emotions themselves. Being able to actually disconnect from the emotion is difficult and this can influence behavior as well as emotions.

Making any decision can be something that's more challenging to an HSP because they're constantly weighing up the options. They're thinking about things that are on a much deeper level than their counterparts, making them a lot slower to come up with a definitive answer or solution.

As deep thinkers, Highly Sensitive Persons will often shrink back into their safe space to consider everything before coming back after a challenge. It's not just obstacles and challenges in their own lives that affect them, but it's also what's happening in the lives of those around them. They continue to mull things over in their minds constantly (Bradberry, 2016).

Chapter 6:

EQ Awareness Strategies

"Until you make the unconscious conscious, it will direct your life and you will call it fate."
~ *Carl Jung*

Becoming More Self-Aware

HSPs can be effective by relying on emotional intelligence. There are various strategies that they can incorporate into their lives that will assist them in becoming more in tune with their emotions.

Some of these strategies, according to Drs. Bradberry and Greaves, are as follows:

Agree with the value system that you have identified for your life. If there happens to be anything that you've done recently that doesn't align with this value system, then you're not being true to yourself. This often causes you to react rather than choosing to act from a wise emotional perspective. One of the ways for you to do this effectively is to write your value system down somewhere that you can easily refer to it. If your actions or behavior goes against your value system, then this will create disharmony in your life. They recommend repeating this exercise on a regular basis, searching inwardly for answers, rather than searching outward for answers. This could assist you with improving your level of self-awareness.

Be aware of what your own emotions are currently telling you. As a HSP, you are already adept at searching for things more deeply than those around you. Try and give the emotions you're feeling actual names. Once you're able to do so, you may discover that it's easier to control both the emotion and the behavior that goes along with it. This means having the ability to tie the emotion and the behavior together. Ask yourself how you are feeling your emotions physically. Does anger feel hot, or does it make your palms sweat instead? How about irritation? Where do you feel it physically on your body? As you're able to identify this for yourself, you will discover many new things about yourself that you weren't even aware of before. Are there places in your body that are either feeling tense or uneasy while experiencing certain emotions?

Think about what makes you feel uncomfortable. We are often exposed to certain situations, words, movies, music, and even people that make us feel awkward or uncomfortable. Whatever the reason, pay close attention to see if you can pinpoint what the emotion is that's causing you to feel the way that you do. As with many of these situations, you could benefit from doing some in-depth research into what is causing you to react in a specific way. Once you've analyzed it, write everything down. There are times when we don't understand how we are feeling, or we can't give the emotion we're feeling a name. Through art, music, dance, movies, and other diverse forms of media, we may discover something that resonates within us deeply. Attention should be paid to these emotions especially.

Consider the impact that your emotions have on others. As a Highly Sensitive Person, you are usually good at placing the needs and feelings of others ahead of your own. Consider who else may be directly influenced by your thoughts and actions. It's seldom that any thought, behavior, action, or reaction happens in complete isolation. Some of these effects can be long-lasting and even impact those who you're not aware of. You may not have even considered how far-reaching your decisions or actions may be. Just as skipping pebbles across a pond create ripples at each point the stone touches, we too can create similar ripples with those around us. Whenever you're in doubt of whether to create some waves of your own, only do so when absolutely necessary.

Try to identify the beginning of a thought process that leads to an action and consider your behavior. Are there any emotional triggers that have set you off or caused you to act in a certain way? One of the best ways to do this is by looking at the big picture rather than the nitty-gritty details. How many times do we end up getting caught up in small day-to-day emotional details that are unnecessary when we consider a much broader overview? Zoom out from time to time so that you're not constantly focusing on the details. This will help you to see things more clearly and will also assist with emotional overload that's not necessary.

Because we're human, we try to steer as clear as possible from anything that's going to make us feel uncomfortable. We don't want to admit to experiencing negative or bad emotions. In all honesty, we need to be able to work through each of these emotions effectively in order to grow. Shying away from them isn't going to make the feelings disappear. We only find the tools and the strength necessary for coping with these emotions as we face them head on. Whether it's admitting to the fact that we have flaws in our character, or learning to apologize to those around us, it's important to figure out how to process this information and work through it as quickly as possible. This is what will get us through to the end.

Understand where good moods come from so that when these moods suddenly appear irrationally, you will immediately be able to understand and accept this. Happy hormones such as adrenaline and cortisol assist in heightening our moods. These can cause us to make some heady decisions that we may regret later. Understand the difference between unrealistic euphoria and a normal good mood. Whenever you're in one of these heightened moods, avoid the temptation to buy things on impulse. This could lead to buyer's remorse once you receive the bill. Understand the difference between how you feel based on the various emotions that you may be experiencing.

Handling stressful situations as soon as they happen. The only way to work through these situations is being able to identify symptoms of stress and the emotions they evoke. The current lifestyle we're living at the moment causes an insane amount of stress which manifests in different ways within the body. For some it is fatigue, and for others, it may be aches and pains. You know yourself better than anyone else. Because of this, you should be able to tell when you are feeling overwhelmed by stress. What coping mechanisms do you employ when you're under stress? Whether you need a vacation, or somewhere to just rejuvenate and recharge your batteries allowing you to deal with the stress, it's important to figure out what you need to do.

Discover what bad mood(s) you're dealing with and identify the cause, whether it's someone in particular, an event, or just an emotion you're dealing with. Try to trace this emotion back to its source so that you can better understand it. Accept that because something has set off a bad mood, you have the strength and potential to change it. You don't need to be stuck in that place indefinitely. You have complete control over your emotions and can shift out of your bad mood as quickly as you got there.

Part of really being able to understand your emotions comes from being able to journal how you feel. Because you're dealing with something that's intangible, by writing things down, the intangible can actually become tangible. You can also then get a much better handle on your emotions. Journaling often allows you to put into writing emotions that you battle to find words for. It's important to find words to describe what you are going through. Keep your journal writing as a habit and whenever there seems to be something that's difficult or challenging to deal with, pull out your journal and pen and spend some alone time offloading on the blank pages. Try to write in your journal habitually, not just when you are feeling challenged. The most important part of the process is being able to identify your emotions in your journal. Don't limit what you write about, as it's the only way to get to the heart of what's really moving you emotionally.

Recognize your emotions by looking in the mirror. What is your daily appearance telling the world about how you're feeling on the inside? Bradberry and Greaves indicate that when we don't care what we look like, how we carry ourselves, how we speak, or how we treat ourselves and those around us, we have probably given up. What sort of atmosphere is your mood currently creating with those around you? The way you dress and carry yourself often sends messages to others about how we're feeling. We should constantly monitor what we look like, how we sound, and the micro expressions and visual cues we're sending during our communications with those we come into contact with.

Asking others for feedback is an excellent way to broaden our narrow perspective of how we think we're working through something. Our own perspective is always limited and fairly biased in favor of ourselves. Being able to hear from some impartial third parties may be just what you need in order to begin to understand what's setting us off (triggers), and what's keeping you in a specific emotional state. Feedback is a powerful way to discover that big-picture-thinking, bird's eye view. It's being able to see yourself as others see you, rather than looking at yourself only through your own eyes. This allows others to communicate what you may need to improve on from a third-party perspective.

Similar to mindfulness techniques, stop labeling your emotions as positive or negative. Allow them to just be, without passing any judgment over them. Once you label your emotions as positive or negative, it becomes more difficult for you to understand them. This prevents you from moving forward and learning from each of them. It's quite normal for us to want to label things as hot or cold, black or white, good or bad—what happens when we do this though, is that we prevent our own personal progress from taking place.

Before acting or reacting, stop and ask yourself who you are planning on doing what you are about to do. It's important to be able to understand why you do what you do when it comes to emotions. When we become truly self-aware, we can begin to discover where the well-spring of our emotions are based. When you are suddenly overwhelmed by an emotion, or you feel happiness, joy, peace, or anger for no apparent reason, stop and try to discover the reason for the emotion happening to you in the first instance. There's a reason for every single emotion that we ever have. When we can understand what causes the emotion, we can learn to control that emotion and everything it brings along with it (Bradberry & Greaves, 2009).

Becoming More Socially Aware

HSPs should be excellent in this role because of their heightened intuition. They are not only able to feel the emotions of others, but often know what's happening in an environment just by being able to assess the mood. The secret to being able to do this successfully lies in your ability to look outward at the world and those around you, rather than inward at your own emotions. Social awareness is knowing exactly what to say at the right time and to whom.

Becoming socially aware can take a lot of time and practice, or it could come more naturally, as with Highly Sensitive Persons. You are already in a place where you observe everything around you, absorbing it like a sponge. You pick up on subtleties such as a change in the tone of someone's voice, their body language, or a specific "tell" that they might have whenever they're stretching the truth.

Once again, we turn to the expert authors of *Emotional Intelligence 2.0* to discover what they have to say about becoming more socially aware as an emotional intelligence skill. Bradberry & Greaves offer the following insights:

Abandon the note-taking habit at meetings altogether. The reason for this is that it is difficult to multitask effectively. When you're actively taking notes during the course of a meeting, you're not paying attention to what's happening during the meeting on an emotional scale. You are not watching for body language or shifts in mood that may be triggered by something specific. There's usually someone who happens to be taking notes of what is discussed during the meeting and these notes are commonly distributed. You know this already, so there's no need for you to actually be taking notes (unless you happen to be the secretary). To be socially aware, means paying close attention to facial expressions or changes in the tone of voices. This can only occur when you are fully engaged with what is happening during meetings.

The best way for you to check whether you've assessed the accuracy of a situation is simply to ask. You may come across someone who seems miserable. You can simply confirm your assessment of the situation by asking them whether something has happened that has caused them to look sad. We aren't always able to be totally accurate in our assessments of situations and people. Whenever you are in doubt, it's sometimes best to simply ask if you feel comfortable doing it.

As you begin to hone your social awareness skills, you will learn to assess the mood of a room. You can do this by paying close attention by scanning the entire area to understand what people are doing. Are they communicating? What is their body language telling you? Are they animated in the way they're communicating with each other or are they more subdued? Is the mood in the room one that's exciting, or is it more somber? How does the mood make you feel? This should give you greater social awareness insight into the overall mood.

Consider the different cultural practices in the workplace. There are often unwritten rules for every organization. It may be that there are individuals within the organization who have cultural differences that are not the same as your own. Social awareness involves being aware of these differences and being able to work effectively despite having a different belief system. You may be employed as part of a team where cultural diversity exists. This is an important component when it comes to the success of the team as is meeting operational and organizational objectives. Discover what these differences are and be sure to show each of your colleagues the respect they deserve. If rules within your business organization don't clearly state anything regarding company culture, don't assume that these don't exist. They're there, and they may just take a while to unearth.

Declutter your internal space. Let's face it, we have internal voices screaming for attention inside our heads constantly. When we're supposed to be paying attention during a conversation, how often are we actually listening to what the individual has to say? Do we give them our full attention, or are we listening while thinking about how we are going to respond? The latter is most often the case. We don't pay close enough attention to the person we're supposed to be communicating with. Becoming socially aware when we have so many voices going on in our heads can be challenging. We need to learn to silence them and also to become active listeners, allowing others to finish speaking, rather than just jumping in with a response before the person has finished communicating with us.

Fine-tune listening skills by directing all of your concentration toward the person who is speaking. Pay close attention to everything they're saying, in every way, including their facial expressions, to their body language, and micro-expressions. What message are they sharing with you? Is there something that is implied, but not being included vocally? Can you read something between the lines? Does the tone of voice and facial expressions of the individual delivering the message match the message being delivered? Is your mind clear of distractions, or is your mind racing away with other thoughts instead of being fully present in the moment?

Nothing will do more for your social awareness skills than getting to know people's names. When you think about where your name comes from and how important it is to you as an individual, then you can understand how great your remembering it makes them feel. Knowing that you remember them can score you major points when it comes to social awareness. Even if you have the memory of a goldfish and battle to remember a name, try and come up with creative ways to imprint the name on your brain. Some people try to associate the name with pictures. You can also ask them how to spell their name as a way to remember. Practice repeating their name several times before you approach the individual for your formal greeting.

Practice identifying emotional intelligence in movies. This is a great way to bolster your social intelligence skills. There are several reasons for this. The first is that art imitates reality. What's portrayed in the movies is an example of what life is all about with the exception that it's usually larger than life. For a Highly Sensitive Person, this is a great way to practice sharpening your emotional intelligence skills without becoming fully invested emotionally. You don't need to actually be dealing with the emotional situation because it's not real. You can, however, identify different moods, facial expressions, and cues given off by actors and actresses as they interact through various scenes in the movies. Another benefit is being able to watch something more than once to identify those very subtle nuances that you may have missed the first time around.

Moments are magical right now. Don't worry about what happened yesterday, as it's in the past, and don't worry about tomorrow because the future is not guaranteed for any of us. Be in the present moment. This is something that you're able to control. Try to live and be present through every part of each day. When you are at home, be present with your spouse, your loved ones, or your family.

If you are attending a business meeting, give it all of your attention and focus your mind on that specific moment. Being present will ensure that there are no mental disruptions and that you're not hanging onto things that have already happened. You can do nothing to alter any past experiences (which we often spend countless hours beating ourselves up about). There's also no point in trying to plan too far in advance, because anything can happen to change the course of your life in the future.

Be well prepared when attending social gatherings. The aim is to be prepared for almost any eventuality that may take place. From the moment you confirm your attendance, you should begin to plan. If you've committed to take something to the event, make a note of it. One of the best methods is to keep a small notebook that you can carry around with you. If there are things that you know you need to accomplish at the event, then make sufficient notes that will remind you what you need to do. By having the notebook as a backup with a list of things you need to do, you can actually concentrate on the social gathering in such a way that you are aware of what is happening around you. Obviously, it is impossible for you to predict exactly what will occur at this event; however, if you need to accomplish something for yourself and you're aware of it from the time you accept the invitation, then it's best to write it down. The beauty of having a small notebook is that you can carry it around with you and check things off as you accomplish them.

Get into the habit of watching people. A great way to do this is by sitting quietly at your favorite coffee shop. Monitoring other customers or people within the mall will provide you with an excellent resource of individuals to watch. You can easily hone your own social awareness skills by quietly watching the world go by. Examples might include couples holding hands, or parents interacting with their children who are trying to assert their independence where the parents aren't giving in. Others may include friendly boutique assistants, or shoppers meandering through various aisles in larger chain stores. Pay attention to the pace at which they are moving. Are they likely to be on vacation? Is the petite blonde merely grabbing a quick bite to eat during her lunch hour? Making a regular habit of observing those around you will make you more socially aware in general.

Study body language thoroughly from head to toe to gain some interesting insight into the unspoken. It's not only poker players who can benefit from studying hand movements, the directions of the eyes, how people position their bodies, or whether arms or hands are folded (are they closed off to you or not). Certain individuals can be classified as being shifty or shady characters simply by studying their body language for a while. One of the first places to start is the eyes, for they truly are the windows to the soul. There's a lot that can be learned by looking into a person's eyes. Are they prepared to maintain eye contact with you or not? When in doubt, if someone is batting their eyelids or their eyes are moving back and forth, chances are that they are being dishonest.

Life is constantly abuzz with activities and things that demand our time and attention. Social awareness takes practice, as does building the skill necessary to be able to recognize people's behavioral patterns and their moods. Instead of rushing through your day as you normally would, take a brief detour along the way. Spend some time just watching how people act or react. Find a bench where you can quietly sit and observe peoples' faces, their expressions, body language, and interactions with one another. By setting aside several minutes every couple of weeks, after a few months, you should be well-versed in the way that people behave. This is what social awareness is all about. You can mix it up a bit from time to time;

some days try and identify the different moods around various people. Another idea may be to analyze and identify characteristics of relationships.

Consider your timing when approaching someone. Be sensitive to things that may be going on in their lives at the time, rather than being selfish by demanding your own way, or for your own needs to be met. An example of this would be if one of your colleagues is dealing with the loss of a family member and you happen to be more interested in monthly figures for a report that's due. Showing empathy and understanding first and foremost is what's called for in this type of situation. Once you know that your colleague is in the right frame of mind, you can cautiously approach them for the monthly figures. You may even want to offer to assist them if these figures are not ready. Someone going through a bereavement is definitely not going to be able to think straight for a while, especially if it was someone extremely close to them.

Think about what it would be like to take a walk in the other person's shoes for a while. This is a technique that's often used in the film and acting community. For an actor or actress to get into character, they often do a deep investigation of the type of character that the individual would be like. The interesting feedback or observation that comes from this exercise is that an actor or actress often reports back that they suddenly have a greater respect toward the type of person who they portrayed. When it comes to social awareness, putting yourself in the other person's shoes is as close as you can get to correctly assessing and interpreting another person's behavior.

Develop a life-saving question especially for those moments when the conversation seems as though it's dead in the water. It doesn't matter whether the question diverts the conversation completely. This would be used to break long, awkward silences that occur occasionally during conversations. Anything that's longer than 10 seconds can seem like forever, especially when nobody has anything to say. Some questions can include queries about current events. Steer clear of religion, politics, or any other controversial topics that may make speaking to one another even more difficult. Social awareness means being prepared for any eventuality, even if this means inviting someone else to join the conversation or excusing yourself in a professional manner. Depending on what the occasion is, you might want to prepare a couple of suitable questions surrounding the event just in case you find yourself facing someone with whom you're battling to connect. For a Highly Sensitive Person, this may feel as if there's something wrong with you. There isn't—it happens at times. The best thing you can do is to have several of these conversation starters or go-to questions planned beforehand.

Chapter 7:
EQ Management Strategies

"Emotional intelligence is the ability to sense, understand, and effectively apply the power and acumen of emotions as a source of human energy, information, connection, and influence."
~ Robert K. Cooper, PhD.

How to Master Self-Management

There's much more to being able to manage yourself and your emotions effectively than just breathing deeply or counting to 10 before you react (although these are still valid techniques when used correctly). It's also more than being reactive to things immediately as soon as they happen. Self-management involves assessing a situation intelligently, without falling to pieces, or erupting at the first sign of drama. Mastering self-management requires you to have the potential and capacity to work through a series of emotions in such a way that you manage them effectively, rather than having them manage you. Many of the techniques listed here involve brain and body chemistry and how they affect the body. Learning to use them effectively will help us to discover self-management techniques. Here are some creative examples of how to master the art of self-management combined with emotional intelligence:

Be gracious and accept that your life is about to change. By using self-management strategies, discipline, and hard work, be prepared to receive the gift of change that's about to take place in many areas of your life. Change can be extremely powerful when it's embraced as being something positive. Too often, we anticipate that the future holds nothing but challenges and disappointment for us, yet when that's exactly what we receive, we are surprised. All that has happened is that what we have anticipated has materialized in our present reality. To break this cycle, we need to believe that change is not only possible, but that it will happen if we are positive and anticipate it occurring.

When you learn how to breathe correctly, you can regain control of your emotions. Very few individuals breathe to the point where they fill their lungs to capacity. Instead, they take small, shallow breaths which deprive the brain of much needed oxygen. You can tell when you've filled your lungs to capacity—your stomach extends outwards and the skin becomes tight. Your breaths should be slow and full, inhaling through the nose and exhaling through your mouth until your lungs are completely deflated. If you're feeling as though your emotions have run away from you, try breathing deeply for several long, full breaths. They should be performed well enough for you to begin feeling the calming effects of oxygen traveling to the brain. This will immediately bring your emotions under your control, increasing self-management and presenting a clearer head.

Sleep is an important factor when it comes to effective functioning. It's important to get a grip on your sleep hygiene. One of the things that needs to be self-managed is getting sufficient sleep at nighttime. There are a number of ways that this can be accomplished. Ensure that you spend between 20 and 30 minutes in the sunlight before midday. This simple exercise helps to regulate your body's internal clock and makes evening sleep more successful. The next thing is to ensure that your bed is used purely for sleeping in. Avoid working in bed, watching movies, or surfing the internet. Your system requires a minimum of two hours where there's been no screen interference before sleeping. This goes for checking social media as well. Be sure that you set a specific cut-off time for electronic/television/media activity daily and be sure to stick with it. Aim for getting a solid eight hours of sleep. Surprisingly, the older we get, the less sleep we actually need; however, start with eight hours each night and see how much better you feel about yourself in the morning. One final note when it comes to sleep—avoid caffeine at nighttime, as this will interfere with the quality of your sleep.

Rediscover the importance of being able to count to 10! Whenever something frustrates you to the point where you feel close to exploding, take a few moments, and a couple of deep breaths and count to 10 under your breath while inhaling deeply through your nose and exhaling through your mouth. You should find that this brings immediate release to pent-up frustrations or emotions. Often, you may reach five and be feeling calmer and more composed, ready to take on the world. At other times, you may surpass the numerical benchmark without feeling any better at all. The point of the exercise is to distract yourself from the frustration long enough to move forward and past whatever is irritating you.

Create an emotion and reason list whenever you're faced with tough judgment calls. You may wish to look at this as heart versus head, or a list of pros and cons. Whatever you want to call it, the reality is that you will be taking the time to draw up a list of all of the emotions you're feeling and exactly what they're telling you to do, versus a list where the brain is in control. There are no right or wrong answers here. There will be times when reasoning with your emotions is the right way to go; however, there may be other times when pure rationale is a better option. Self-management would allow you to gain these skills and use them whenever you're faced with a challenging situation. Don't simply jump in with both feet immediately. Consider your options and look at what the list is telling you to do, using both logic and emotion. The two need to be considered together.

One way to improve yourself each and every day is by choosing to learn something new from everyone you meet. This doesn't need to be anything grandiose or major, as the aim should be to make every contact and connection with another human being as productive and beneficial as possible. Albert Einstein maintained that anyone was able to be a genius if they dedicated just 10 minutes daily to a specific subject matter for a period of one year. Imagine how much you could grow within a lifetime when you begin with one year or 365 days and 365 new concepts or ideas. Compounded over the next year, 730 new concepts over two years, and so on. If you meet more than one person daily on average, the above figures could be pretty conservative if your goal is to successfully learn at least one new thing from each encounter. Imagine the possibilities.

One of the best ways to achieve the goals that you set for yourself is to make people aware of them. They can act as our cheerleaders, coaches, goalkeepers, and motivators, especially when we hit a slump. Keeping ourselves motivated all the time can be heavy going, especially when we come up against obstacles. By sharing your goals with a variety of people, you can arrange to check in with them via a reporting mechanism. Another important form of self-management should be a reward system. Whenever you achieve any of your goals or milestones, you should be appropriately rewarded. Similarly, in the event that you miss doing what you've set out to do, a penalty system could encourage you to do better next time.

It is impossible to keep going physically and mentally day in and day out. It's vital to schedule suitable time to recharge your mental batteries. There are a number of ways to do this successfully from reading good books to listening to positive, uplifting audiobooks. Set aside time for daily meditation, yoga, or other forms of restoration. Whatever works for you, set aside this time aside and try not to deviate from it. It needs to become a habit for it to become an effective tool in your self-management strategy.

I'm sure you will agree that we live in an ever-changing fast-paced world. It's not likely to slow down anytime soon, either. The average individual has between 30,000 to 50,000 random thoughts daily that come and go, passing through the brain. Some of these are important for problem solving, while others are exactly that—random. Rather than trying to come up with a method of sorting through the plethora of thoughts roaming through your mind, put pen to paper every time there happens to be a thought passing through your brain that warrants problem solving. The next step is to set aside a specific time when you can work through your list for a set period of time. This will become your plan for problem-solving. By setting aside a daily fixed time, your problems won't build to the point where they overwhelm you. At the same time, don't sit attempting to resolve your problems for longer than the time you've allocated. Any unresolved problems should then move on to the following day, and so on.

Whenever you feel that you're facing a challenge or something that needs to be decided on urgently, one of the best strategies is to give it 24 hours. Don't allow yourself to be pushed into making any hasty move or decision to please anyone else. Whenever there is something bothering you, take some time to sleep on it. Give yourself the extra time before racing into something which you might regret later. By giving yourself the gift of extra time, you are essentially managing your emotions effectively. You are allowing your thoughts to clear sufficiently to make a decision that's going to be better than one that's crafted based on a knee-jerk response.

Practice happiness by smiling more. Even faking a smile can initially prove to substantially lighten your mood. One of the ways to do this is by reading material with humor, such as comic books, or books filled with humor and wit that you know are going to make you smile or laugh. Because your brain is influenced by the work of your muscles, you can literally trick yourself into feeling better by forcing a great big grin. This works out especially well if you work in an environment such as customer service, as your mood will translate to your actions. By faking a broad smile all day long, your mood will shift, and you should soon begin feeling lighter and more relaxed.

One of the best ways to deal with emotions and challenges is by speaking with a mentor. This individual should not be someone you know extremely well, and especially not a spouse or family member. Instead, they should be someone who knows you on a professional level, without being exposed to any other emotional baggage that you may be carrying around with you. You will want your mentor to be impartial and be able to give you sound business advice, without you having to face constant scrutiny or judgment in other areas of your life. This is not to say that you should give yourself a pass on those issues that may be holding you back. There's a time and a place for discussing these things and if you feel that you need professional help, then contact a professional medical practitioner who may be able to refer you to the right kind of therapy or counseling. In the meantime, continue working with your mentor for assistance in reaching your business and/or career objectives.

Another self-management strategy that you can always count on is to have your physical behavior, thoughts, and actions remain in agreement. This means that they're constantly aligned with one another and in perfect harmony. This could be anything from the way you speak to the tone of your voice. The common term for this is synchronicity. We often ensure that our computer and phone are perfectly synchronized, meaning that they work in tandem with one another and both have exactly the same information available. Your body also needs to be operating this way to get the most from personal management.

Turn the volume right down when it comes to negative self-talk. We all make mistakes on a daily basis and still have much to learn. There's little value to be gained from berating or running ourselves down in front of others. We should watch what we say and how we say those things to ourselves. Accept that perfection is something that nobody is able to achieve. Be kind to yourself, instead of constantly berating yourself for making mistakes. Remember that you are human, and along with this, comes a lot of trial and error.

There are another two strategies when it comes to self-talk that can be explored. One is accepting blame and accountability for the things that we do get wrong from time to time, as this gives you an opportunity to be able to grow as an individual. If however, you are assuming the blame or responsibility as a means of keeping the peace, this is never going to work productively. The second area requires being realistic about mistakes as and when they are made. Don't automatically dump all the blame on yourself as a way to side-step real issues. The days of stating that you "could have done it this way," or "it may have been better being done another way" are in the past and there's little you can do about it other than learning from experience. Choose a different strategy and tactic when it comes to the constant voice that's rambling on and on in your head.

Identify someone who you believe is an experienced self-manager and schedule a meeting with them. This should ideally be someone who has strengths in the emotional intelligence area where you have weaknesses. You cannot gain any new insights into developing habits that can benefit you and those around you from anyone other than someone who possesses these things as strengths.

One of the first, and most important keys to self-management strategies in emotional intelligence is to surround yourself with those who have strengths where you have limitations. Don't be afraid to tell them why you want to tap into their skills. You will no doubt discover that they are more than willing to mentor you in their area of strength. Whatever you do, make the best use of their time. Don't waste their time or let them down. If you've committed to working with them, appreciate that they are professionals and have additional demands on their time. Do what you commit to doing.

Visualization is the secret to being successful. The reason for this is that neural pathways in the brain can only be developed through visualization. No number of written goals will have the same effect as being able to visualize success with a picture of success. It's not just useful when it comes to the ability to achieve our short- and long-term goals, it's also a really great tool to have when preparing for an important presentation, a speech, or a social gathering. You can become all hyped up by the emotional demands being placed on you. Through self-management, you are the only one who holds the power to either tone these up or down.

Mastering Relationship Management

Developing and mastering relationships can be hard work. Nobody said that it was going to be easy. Initially when you meet someone, everything seems to be blissful and easy. Yet, at some point, there will be a change felt. Things that you found endearing in the beginning are starting to annoy you. This annoyance can easily force the relationship onto rocky ground unless you are able to implement and use some serious relationship management skills. I'd like to point out that all relationships require work, no matter how long people have been together or how long you may have worked at the same organization.

We all need to be prepared to learn more about relationship management and how this single emotional intelligence characteristic actually relies on all of the other three characteristics, namely self-awareness, self-management, and social awareness, to be effective. This is the reason for it being saved for last as a skill that you need to master. According to Bradberry & Greaves, all of the emotional intelligence skills can be learned and mastered through practice. Self-awareness requires being able to feel and define the emotions that you are currently experiencing. Social awareness is the practice of using these skills to understand the emotions, mood, and atmosphere in an environment.

This may take some practice, but let's acknowledge that other people have emotions that can derail them as well. HSPs are not the only ones who feel things deeply. Part of social management is being able to tune into the emotions of others and offering them emotional support by identifying with what they are feeling. There may be a lot that they are not saying, but their mood, their eyes, and their body language are communicating loud and clear. Be compassionate and empathetic with them, rather than aloof or telling them to "get it together." Remember how you would feel whenever someone gave you that practical advice as a coping mechanism for your problems? Show those around you that you genuinely care about them by taking the time to actively listen to what they have to say.

Foster a genuine open-door policy where staff members feel that they are welcome to stop by your office to discuss anything and everything (obviously, within reason). You want your team to feel that they are important and if something is bugging them, that they can knock on your door and there will be a guaranteed, interested, listening ear available. Many managers claim that they have this policy in place and yet, leave their employees hanging out to dry when times get tough. The manager who has true empathy for his team will be prepared to hear all sides of an argument before taking the facts into consideration. They are able to separate themselves from making irrational decisions because of hierarchical set-ups within business organizations. Having an open-door policy that is genuine can go a long way toward healthy communication.

Prevent yourself from sending out mixed messages in the form of what your body language is saying versus what is coming out of your mouth. It is challenging to stop your body from displaying certain emotions because it habitually displays cues and micro-cues automatically. By sending these messages, managers and those communicating, may receive incorrect signals which becomes confusing for them. We cannot always control the signals sent by our bodies immediately after bad news is received, a difficult conversation is had, an altercation is experienced, or similar. Should you find yourself in this kind of situation, sometimes the best way to deal with it is to be honest with your audience to confirm that any irrational vibe is a result of something else completely.

In social management, being open and curious is one of the skills you must bring to the table. The truth is that, while you may think that disclosing personal information about yourself or learning personal information about others can feel like too much information, it could potentially save a lot of misunderstandings later on. Take the example where you don't drink or smoke for health and medical reasons. Yet, there are others within the organization who regularly go out for drinks after work and often invite you to join them. Once they understand that you have a medical condition that prevents you consuming any alcohol, they may be more understanding and even supportive. They may begin to provide a whole host of non-alcoholic beverages for you at work events. A little understanding goes a long way.

Be acutely aware that you are constantly either building trust or breaking it down. While trust always takes an extensive amount of time to nurture, develop, and build, it is fragile and can be destroyed in an instant. With this in mind, you need to be overly cautious of how you treat this gift that's given to you by those you work with, those you work for, those you love, and those who love you. It's not often that we consider how valuable something as fragile as trust can be. We need to protect this trust as much as possible so that we honor and respect the person who trusts us.

Avoid mirroring someone's behavior on the phone or in person as this can often end in disaster. Complement the person's emotions or situation instead. This means that you need to demonstrate exceptional listening skills to express the right amount of compassion and empathy, attention and understanding, and service delivery. As a social management tool, this will allow you to prove that you understand exactly what the individual on the other end requires and that you will give them exactly what they are asking for. It's more than just being polite; it's being able to understand the customer on the other end of the phone line, what they require, and then providing it to them.

There will always be someone in the workplace with whom you don't particularly enjoy working. Don't keep putting off the inevitable because, at some stage or another, you will probably be thrown into the same ring. You will either be assigned to work together on a project or be forced to co-manage a group of people. If you've been working for the same organization for a while, you're extremely lucky that you've managed to steer clear as long as you have done. In reality, the time is definitely going to come where you're going to be pushed out of your comfort zone directly into the firing line of this individual. This is where sound social awareness skills come into play. You may have to swallow your pride and practice some of the techniques mentioned above where you do your best to find out as much as you possibly can to foster a good working arrangement. Practice virtually standing in their shoes for a while. What does it feel like for them? What obstacles do they have, or have they had to overcome in order to get to where they are now? I'm not saying that you're immediately going to be able to sit around the same cozy campfire, but you definitely will be able to muddle through a project together.

Discover the way you communicate with others by completing a formal assessment. In a journal or on a piece of paper, draw a line down the middle of the page. On the left-hand side, write down how you think others perceive your communication. Is it quirky, direct, troublesome, irritating, or illegible? Then, think about how you perceive your communication to others to be. Do you believe that you communicate directly, rationally or too directly for sensitive readers? In order to find common ground, weigh both sides against one another. Choose three positive characteristics of your communication that you can continue to build on. Using the same document, identify three weak areas that you can eliminate from your communication. Use three positives to enhance your communication, and three negatives to hone your communication skills.

By explaining your decisions to people or groups of people, rather than simply announcing them, you can get a chance to win them over to your side. If you run roughshod over people, without any forethought or afterthought, you can be left wondering whether you have, in fact, made the right decision after all. By explaining decisions and the reasoning behind them, you can avoid people wondering and can have them be reassured. Understanding the decision-making process makes it easier for people to accept the decision. It may also open the lines of communication for sharing different ideas or solutions to problems that may not have been previously explored.

Losing your temper is to be avoided. When anger, a powerful emotion, is expressed in a healthy way, it can be extremely valuable. You need to use negative emotions appropriately, rather than as and when it suits you. Even when justified, vent if you must and then leave it be. It doesn't help to remain frustrated or angry for an extended period of time. Your aim should be to address the situation or event that caused the anger and then move on.

Excellent manners make the man, or woman. Society has become desensitized to language primarily because everything is so fast-paced and hectic. The one thing that seems to have been lost or left behind appears to be decent manners. The plain and simple, "Thank you," "Please," "You're welcome," and "It's a pleasure" seem to be missing from everyday speech. It may seem like a small thing (which it is, really), yet few people use good manners. It seems like it's every man for himself and nobody seems to care anymore. If you can adopt an attitude of respect from the perspective that you treat everyone exactly the same way as you would like to be treated, then there is some hope of resurrecting the old tradition of good manners.

Find ways to deal with difficult conversations. They are always going to come up in business, no matter how long you've been at it. Rather than side-stepping issues, face them head on as and when they occur. If you must discipline staff, then be sensitive to their needs, while being professional enough to effectively communicate your message to the parties concerned. Speak directly so that there can be no misunderstanding or miscommunication. Be sure that there is a clear understanding each step of the way, rather than reaching the end of the communication only to discover that they did not understand you at the beginning. Avoid ambiguity. Use all of the emotional intelligence skills you have available to you to communicate professionally and effectively.

Ask for feedback on a regular basis and pay attention while receiving it because it's going to make you a better individual. It's true that none of us like to hear where we're failing, where we need to improve, or things we need to stop doing to improve our lives and the lives of those around us. We do need to hear these things though, and to pay specific attention if we want to grow and thrive as individuals. Asking for feedback on a regular basis means that change can happen consistently, rather than all at once where it's a major shock to the system. People who you should be asking for feedback from include not only those with whom you work, clients, colleagues, and associates, but family members, loved ones, and those we care about. Sound social management comes from the ability to be successful with all interactions and not just those that we think are important. It's viewing all forms of communication and interaction from a holistic perspective.

Even the simplest random acts of kindness can go a long way to boost morale. Along with the fast pace of society, it often appears as though nobody cares about whether you are doing a good job or not. This is a generalization because there are many managers and team leaders who consistently express their sincere appreciation for work being done. That being said, there are just as many who don't care at all. They believe that those working for them actually owe them something. There's nothing wrong with expressing additional appreciation whenever it is due. Two small words—"Thank you"—cost nothing to say, yet they can make a difference to how well a task is performed.

CHAPTER 8:

ANXIETY AND THE HIGHLY SENSITIVE PERSON

"Sensitive people like a slower pace of life. We like pondering all our options before making a decision and regularly reflecting on our experiences. We hate busy schedules and rushing from one event to the next."
~ Jenn Granneman

Society has become frenetic when it comes to pace. We have everything from fast cars, supercomputers, fast foods, and anything else that you could possibly imagine. Almost everywhere you look there are things that are supposed to make our lives easier. While for the non-HSP, all these things may seem to indicate progress, for a Highly Sensitive Person, it represents additional demands on their time. Decisions need to be made a lot quicker, each of these adding to the anxiety that the HSP already feels building around them.

For the HSP, just driving to work or school can already be stressful with all the traffic, loud noises, blaring music, and honking horns. Each of these plays on the senses of the HSP, causing them to feel like they're about to overload and burn out at any moment. All of this is going on before the day has really started. In the event that this has been the start of the HSPs day, there are a number of things that need to take place for the Highly Sensitive Person to survive.

Dealing with Anxiety as an HSP

According to Ted Zeff, PhD, in his book, *The Highly Sensitive Person's Survival Guide: Essential Skills for Living Well in an Overstimulated World*, if you were a non-HSP about to face a heart attack due to your living conditions, in most instances, you would take the counsel offered by a medical practitioner to change your life immediately. Similarly, as an HSP, there are a number of things that you can begin doing immediately that can make your life a whole lot easier to handle. Some of these things are detailed in the next paragraphs.

Changing your attitude toward things going on in your environment is something that can be extremely beneficial. If you believe that your day is going to be filled with anxiety and stress, then guess what? Chances are that you will be right. Whether you believe in it or not, we attract certain things into our lives every moment of every day. When we believe that we are able to cope with additional stress in our lives, we will discover that the coping mechanisms are there.

Does this mean that stress will automatically disappear from our lives? Absolutely not! This means that we will have better coping mechanisms in place, so that we no longer feel totally overwhelmed by the demands of the day. Each of the techniques can be adapted to meet the needs of your lifestyle immediately. You don't need to make use of every suggestion. Instead, choose those that are going to work for you. You may already be working with some of these (or similar) anxiety interventions—keep at it.

Some of the following recommendations may resonate with you and you may want to add them. My recommendation is to do it slowly, adding one specific thing at a time, measuring whether it works for you or not. Because we are all unique and different, we have different needs as HSPs. This is the reason why some of the techniques will work more effectively than others. The point of each of these items is to assist you in working through anxiety issues that you may be experiencing as an HSP. Should any of these recommendations not work for you, or make you feel greater anxiety than you're already experiencing, abandon it completely and try something else.

Practice deep breathing exercises. We've mentioned this in previous chapters. This is simply a reminder to breathe in deeply through your nose, ensuring that your lungs are filled to capacity. You will be able to tell if you are inhaling fully, as the skin on your stomach will be feeling tight. Slowly exhale through your mouth, forcing all of the air out, ensuring that your lungs are completely empty. Do this whenever you begin feeling anxious. It will restore a sense of peace and calm to your mood almost immediately. Your brain requires a certain amount of oxygen in order to function efficiently. By breathing deeply and filling your lungs to capacity, you are forcing this oxygen to go where it needs to. As you begin doing this on a regular basis, you will notice that you don't only feel calmer, but you feel as though you are able to take on the world. For an HSP, this is an excellent coping mechanism that costs nothing and can be practiced at any time.

Find the best way to calm your senses that are consistently being bombarded by various stimuli from people demanding your attention, loud music, noise from traffic, loud voices, machinery and equipment in the background, and your phone beeping with unread social media notifications. Each demands your immediate undivided attention. In all honesty, how much of the external stimuli is actually really necessary? How much are you able to get rid of so it's no longer demanding your time and attention? One of the best ways to deal with overstimulation of your senses is to unplug from all technology for a while. Not only will this reduce the overstimulation that you're constantly feeling, but it will put you back in the driver's seat. Say "No" to Facebook and other social media demands for a week and notice the difference that it makes in your life.

If you doubt that you can manage for an entire week without being able to connect with others via social media, then learn to set aside a specific time in the day for it (put a time limit on it for 10 or 15 minutes and then be sure to stick with this limit). Switch off all social media notifications so that they're not going to interfere in your day and thus continue to create a sense of overstimulation in your life. For an HSP, such constant interruption can create hyperstimulation that's challenging to cope with.

Discover ways to calm your mind by clearing away the clutter that may be overwhelming your senses. There are a number of ways to do this. The first of these is practicing something known as a brain dump where you take a journal and pen and write down everything that you're currently thinking about. This doesn't need to be a lengthy process, and you can start off by just writing short bullet points for everything that has been on your mind, or that you feel needs to be dealt with. Once you've done this, you will be amazed by how light your mood feels. This is because your mind is no longer weighed down by mental overload and things that you're constantly ruminating about. Rumination means that you are thinking about the same things over and over again, similar to when a hamster is running on a treadmill. The treadmill is stationary and no matter how hard or fast the hamster runs, it never really gets anywhere. Rumination has a similar mechanism. For someone who is an HSP, it is much worse though because the emotional attachment with the rumination process is intense.

Something that HSPs constantly seem to forget is that they always have a choice when it comes to what they are going to let into their thoughts and what they are going to say "No" to. Because thoughts and emotions seem to come from every direction, HSPs often feel as though they're surrounded by too many stimuli. This causes them to feel overanxious. The choice is that they can either try to remove themselves from the stimuli or they can reduce stimulation by toning down its effects. Closing their eyes to limit a visual onslaught or putting on headphones to reduce an auditory attack can be helpful.

Routines Provide Structure

There are two sets of routines that HSPs can establish as part of their lives. The first is an evening routine. Evening routines are designed to reduce as much overstimulation as possible. They should be calming by their nature to assist with sleep patterns. One of the most important things regarding evening routines is that they should be exactly the same seven days a week, not changing over weekends which may throw the entire system out of sync. For the final 30 minutes before the end of the day, the focus should be inwards, rather than outwards. This means that the time spent should be meditative, calming, and free from stimulation. This is where reading could be done, as well as writing in journals and choosing to do things that are relaxing, rather than stimulating.

Examples of things that are relaxing are things like taking a long, relaxing bath, where you can play relaxing music to assist in getting the body into the habit of falling asleep.

Things to avoid in the evenings includes television shows where there is a lot of action, violence, or visual stimulation. If there happens to be something that you'd really like to watch, record the show or set up another more suitable time earlier in the day to watch, rather than just before you retire for the evening.

Your sleep routine should be exactly the same every day, including weekends. Be sure that you retire at the same time every evening (or as close to the same time as possible) as this will allow you to get into a regular sleeping pattern. Don't expect this to happen immediately, it will take a while for your body to get into the habit of being able to sleep for the right amount of time and being awake for the same number of hours each day.

A morning routine would consist of different things, but could be just as important for you to successfully deal with your anxiety issues. Consider getting up earlier each morning and setting aside specific time for things such as meditation, relaxation, and exercise. Morning meditation can consist of reading uplifting books or motivational material to start your day. By waking up earlier, you can take time to prepare for the day ahead of you rather than rushing to get to work or to accomplish whatever your specific plans are for the day. Taking the time, either the night before or first thing in the morning to schedule your day correctly, brings a certain degree of calm. You can also begin your day by getting some exercise such as yoga or Tai Chi. These exercises allow you to become centered physically and mentally, becoming prepared for the day. Each of these exercises teaches you to breathe properly as well.

The next step in a successful morning routine is setting aside enough time to eat a healthy breakfast. It's believed to be the most important meal of the day. Ensure that you have a hearty breakfast that's not rushed.

Part of not rushing in the morning includes allowing yourself more than enough travel time for your commute into the office. This will allow you to relax throughout your journey, despite others who may be in an impatient rush. As an HSP, you would be more likely to feel the pressure and frustration of being stuck in traffic, or running to catch a bus or train, becoming completely out of breath in the process.

Part of your anti-anxiety process should be learning to separate yourself completely from a situation. You are aiming to reach a positive mental destination rather than taking a negative mental journey.

Taking enough time to create a healthy eating plan will relieve you of unnecessary stress, which is the whole point of gaining control of your emotions. Instead of being an HSP, you can begin to master the art of emotional intelligence. It will assist you in being able to relax, possibly reducing the number of times in a day that you berate yourself.

Another way to deal with anxiety is writing about it. Your journal will soon become one of your best friends.

Overcoming Anxiety with Emotional Intelligence

According to psychotherapist, and award-winning author *of How to Raise a Secure Child - Parenting with Empathy,*

Dr. Erin Leonard, there is a strong connection between emotional intelligence and anxiety. She states that, "Emotional intelligence is not the absence of anxiety, but being able to embrace it." The reason for this is that HSPs are in touch with their emotions and feel things more deeply. This makes them exceptional when it comes to awareness, whether it's themselves, or being aware of the emotions of those around them. Because of this, they are certainly prone to feeling anxiety and possibly, even depression (Leonard, 2020).

When it comes to self-awareness and social awareness, HSPs possess both because they are able to feel compassion and empathy. Depending on the mood and the emotions they pick up from the environment, they are able to place themselves in the situation of those experiencing the emotions. This makes them excellent at reading moods and emotion. The downside when it comes to this is that HSPs could easily form an attachment to others who are experiencing these emotions. This attachment could mean that they naturally reabsorb these emotions. The whole point of these exercises is to help HSPs become stronger and less overwhelmed by the emotions and feelings of others. Always consider this when working with both compassion and empathy.

The Highly Sensitive Person

When you possess high emotional intelligence, you can become comfortable even within your own insecurity. It allows you to manage your emotions in a productive way by being able to name them and work through them. On the other hand, low emotional intelligence suggests that someone who feels threatened by those who can handle their emotions. This, more often than not, contributes to low self-esteem. High emotional intelligence allows you to work through emotions without them having a negative influence on your well-being. It's being aware that the emotions are there and being able to feel them without allowing them to consume you.

Conversely, if you happen to be suffering from low emotional intelligence, you need to sever the ties with these intense emotions because they can contribute to low self-esteem and all of the negative emotions that go along with it.

There's a huge difference between self-confidence and low self-esteem. They are at opposite ends of a spectrum. Low self-esteem could cause you to suffer from feelings of failure, bringing about feelings of jealousy and uncontrolled outbursts. The point is that, at this stage, instead of creating an environment that's win-win, it's one where nobody wins. The situation can often escalate, instead becoming destructive.

When you have healthy emotional intelligence, you can choose to act on a situation rather than reacting. Choosing to react rather than act could exert a negative impact on the HSP and the people who they work with. Having healthy EQ means being able to read situations as they unfold and choosing to act appropriately. It doesn't help to keep negative emotions to yourself because you aren't sure how they will be received. At this point, you should have a complete understanding of the situation and how others are feeling, especially as an HSP. You know emotions better than anyone else and should be able to work with social awareness characteristics to accomplish the very best possible outcome.

Understanding the emotions of others is essential to emotional intelligence. This is where you would use your self-awareness to assess your own status. What is your emotional temperature and temperament? Is your mood going to positively or negatively impact the current situation? As you're performing your self-awareness assessment, this would give you an opportunity to reflect on what's happening with your emotions. We are often reluctant to reflect on what we're doing because it's unpleasant and it can be stressful having to admit to failing in certain areas of our lives. Doing this successfully though is something that is always beneficial. If we are not growing, then we're stagnating. We need to constantly be moving forward.

Self-reflection may mean having to admit to the fact that we have done something wrong. While our actions may not be intentional, being prepared to accept responsibility is a sign of high emotional intelligence. Accountability and owning both mistakes and bad decisions is the difference between someone with low EQ and someone with high EQ. Owning our mistakes and learning from them is one way for us to grow as individuals, as well as in teams within organizations. Emotional intelligence can be used in all areas of our lives. It's not just a business tool, or a personal development tool.

Self-analysis and reflection give you a perfect opportunity to look at how you can improve your current situation, whether this is your behavior or something preventing you from having high emotional intelligence. An example of this would be where you don't believe that anything is your fault, or you're too afraid to accept responsibility for your mistakes. Accepting responsibility and taking ownership provides a unique opportunity for you to learn and grow from the mistakes you've made. Learning and growing means that you can avoid making the same mistakes over and over again. It helps you to see things in a new perspective; one where you can analyze, repair what needs to be repaired, and grow to move forward. Growth comes from self-awareness and being able to look inward.

We've discussed the importance of relationships when it comes to emotional intelligence. This serves as a reminder that emotional intelligence is all about connecting with those around you and developing strong and lasting relationships. As part of this quest, your ability to understand yourself and your emotions helps you to form close connections with others. High self-awareness and emotional intelligence skills provide you with an opportunity to be authentic and accountable. Mistakes made are owned, rather than merely being swept under a rug.

Those with high emotional intelligence and HSPs find it very easy to connect deeply with others. This bond allows

HSPs to become closely connected with one another. Should problems arise in the relationship, this can be extremely traumatic to deal with because they are so firmly attached. Such a loss may leave deep scars and wounds that take a long time to heal. Emotionally adept individuals find severing these links extremely difficult and painful to process. They have often described a loss like this as debilitating. Many try and retreat inwards to where they no longer have to publicly deal with the pain of the failed relationship.

Those with low emotional intelligence can quickly move from one relationship to the next without feeling guilty. They are not as self-aware as their HSP counterparts. They often jump from one shallow relationship to the next, all because they lack sound emotional intelligence and low levels of self-awareness. They cannot identify the feelings we've been talking about. Chances are that these are non-HSPs who aren't in touch with their own feelings, or the feelings of those with whom they're involved. Whether they terminate the relationship, or their partner does, it doesn't take too long for them to recover and move on to the next best thing. Connections are shallow versus the deep connectivity that Highly Sensitive Persons have.

Being in a relationship with someone who has high emotional intelligence definitely has the benefit of them being able to understand your emotions. As a Highly Sensitive Person, you are born with an understanding and ability to connect. Be aware of connecting with those with low emotional intelligence, as they can be the type of individual who is more than likely to break your heart in an instant, without looking back.

For the HSP, anxiety is something that has to be dealt with on a daily basis. There are a wide range of emotions that they experience that all fall within the scope of anxiety. This may be fear, extreme nervousness, panic, stress or worrying about even the smallest things. It may even result in the fight-flight-freeze hormones being released where the HSP is unsure which of the responses is likely to be the best option given the situation. A pulse that quickens, or a heart that beats faster than normal describes physical feelings that a Highly Sensitive Person experiences when they are feeling anxious.

Dr. Elaine Aron states that, "All highly sensitive people worry to some degree. Again, it is part of their survival strategy to consider what the future might bring—to learn from threats and failures. To observe and deeply process the world around them."

Along with these symptoms of anxiety, the HSP may become shy and withdrawn. Dealing with anxiety is one step away from dealing with depression. This needs to be worked through in such a way that you can circumvent these feelings, preventing the onset of depression which is likely to be debilitating. One way to deal with anxiety is making sure that you have enough "alone time" where you can just quietly process whatever is happening around you, rather than leaving it to take root and fester. Hyperstimulation can occur if small triggers that set off anxieties are left unchecked for a given amount of time.

Overstimulation can occur much easier than you would imagine because as an HSP, you are constantly deeply processing what is happening around you. There are a couple of things that can add to you feeling overly anxious as an HSP:

- Considering the welfare of others, before our own.
- Having someone watching you work.

- Not having enough time to practice the "pause and reflect" technique before having to move ahead.
- Placing perfection ahead of yourself as a minimum standard.
- Sensory overstimulation caused by too many people around you.
- Someone demanding more of you than you currently have the capacity to give.

Some of the solutions to these situations can be found by practicing the deep breathing exercises we've already gone through, ensuring that sufficient oxygen fills the lungs to capacity (so that our brains get all the oxygen they need), and releasing the air through the mouth until the lungs are completely deflated. By practicing this breathing technique several times a day (or whenever you feel anxiety coming on), you will quickly notice that your breathing regulates. This lets your heart rate regulate and provides enough oxygen to your brain for you to think clearly.

Other ways to cope are to practice quieting your mind through mindfulness exercises. These are practiced by becoming acutely aware of your thoughts. Think about where they come from, why you're having them, and then let them gently pass over you without holding onto them. Recognize them as being just thoughts. They have no major control over you unless you allow them to.

One other technique that we've briefly mentioned is getting into the habit of unplugging for a while. And yes, I mean your phone! I promise that you will be able to survive without it for as long as you need to. Here are a couple of ideas of when to put your phone away:

- When you go to sleep at night.
- During your commute to the office.
- During lunchtime.
- While you're bathing.
- While you're lined up at a store to pay.

You will discover that you sleep better at night without being tempted to check your phone every so often. Research has been conducted that proves that the brightness of the screen has a negative effect, especially when you are trying to go to sleep. The best ways to do this are to either lock your phone away so that you can't get at it easily or to switch it off all together.

Just as you set limits around your phone time, set boundaries around your personal availability. This is so that you can get as much accomplished as possible, meeting deadlines while dealing with the least amount of stress and anxiety. Think about how often people simply walk into your space or your office at random and strike up a conversation that has no bearing on work. By the time you look at your alarm, an hour has gone by where you've been totally unproductive. I can guarantee that this happens a lot more often than you'd care to admit.

If you're not too sure about this trend that happens in offices globally, pay close attention to your day and note how often this happens. Keep a notebook near you and take note of how much time is being "stolen" from you on a daily basis where you could potentially be productive. Protect this time by placing a "NO ENTRY" sign on your office door. Explain to visitors nicely that you have work that needs to take preference, you have a budget to prepare, reports that need to be compiled and submitted, whatever it is that needs doing. This can be done in a professional way so that they don't feel as though they've been reprimanded like a naughty child. Schedule suitable time(s) when you can catch up after work or outside working hours. Once you've created this block of time, be assertive when it comes to enforcing it.

Pretty soon, others will begin respecting you for your work ethic and they will leave you alone. As an HSP, be prepared for some name-calling once you do go this route. No amount of name calling can hinder your level of productivity in the workplace, if you would set some ground rules.

According to Dr. Aaron, as a Highly Sensitive Person, be aware that you need to also have sufficient time daily, weekly, and seasonally to rest and recover fully to continue being productive. These "down times" may look something like this:

- Daily – 2 hours.
- Weekly – 1 day.
- Seasonally – 1 week.

CHAPTER 9:

WORRY AND THE

HIGHLY SENSITIVE PERSON

"Sensitive people should be treasured. They love deeply and think deeply about life. They are loyal, honest, and true. The simple things sometimes mean the most to them. They don't need to change or harden. Their purity makes them who they are."
~ Kristen Butler

A common characteristic of HSPs is their tendency to constantly worry about everything. Highly Sensitive Persons can worry about the weather, the economy, whether you are actually okay because you seemed a bit down the last time they saw you and a multitude of other things. Part of the reason why Highly Sensitive Persons are extensive worriers is because they were taught to worry from the time they were born. Chances are that one, or even both of their parents, were to be HSPs. This would have meant that they would fuss and fret over their HSP infant. Overanxious parents who cannot leave a baby alone to be able to explore and grow on their own will result in a degree of anxiety within the child.

This only becomes worse as this would have a negative impact on the child by causing sensory overload and consequent overstimulation. This overstimulation is the beginning of a vicious cycle of worry as the child grows older. The reality is that there's no way to protect a child from every single eventuality. Wanting to wrap them up in cotton wool to prevent anything bad from happening to them actually prevents them from experiencing things that would allow them to grow as autonomous individuals.

Worry as a Highly Sensitive Person

This is a natural characteristic or personality trait of an HSP. It doesn't need any form of encouragement from anyone else. Part of what sends Highly Sensitive Persons over the edge with worry is trying to decipher and make sense of their emotions. Too many sounds, people, chatter, lights, and busyness just add to an HSP feeling completely overwhelmed by the world around them. If there's no escape route, or somewhere that they can recharge their batteries, then there's only one outcome that's guaranteed, and that is a sense of overwhelm. It's fine while these highly sensitive individuals are still young enough to retreat somewhere quiet where they feel protected. The problem arises when they're in school, college, or the workplace, and cannot access the same quiet environment.

HSPs can experience a variety of fears and anxieties to varying degrees. The Highly Sensitive Person will often worry over things that they really have no control over which places them under even more stress. Some of the things that can lead to excessive worry are the following:

Daily challenges and obstacles that need to be faced can involve anything from an unforeseen thunderstorm that you hadn't packed an umbrella for, to the economic situation, or the price of crude oil that's going to negatively affect inflation. These concerns become one big vicious circle because there's actually nothing that you can do about any of these things, yet they continue to play on your mind.

Panic attacks are usually caused by worrying about things that you have little or no control over. The above situations are perfect examples of things that you can do nothing about. If you cannot change anything about them, then there's really no point in worrying about them.

You worry about your relationships. These could be your relationships with your spouse or partner, relationships with your children, manager, employer, neighbor, or sometimes even the relationships you have with total strangers. Highly Sensitive Persons don't enjoy people being cruel or unkind to others. You may take exception to someone who's being unkind to animals or children. You are particularly concerned with those who aren't able to defend themselves.

HSPs often worry about meeting pending deadlines. This creates extreme anxiety. Part of not being able to meet an impending deadline may be because you're concerned about everything being perfect. This need for perfection will often cause you to spend longer than necessary working on one aspect of an assignment. HSPs will commonly ruminate for ages about missing deadlines.

Insufficient sleep makes a Highly Sensitive Person more stressed out than they would be under normal circumstances. They need regular and sufficient sleep to cope with the conventional stressors of everyday life. Without sleep, an HSP will usually revert to worry, anxiety, stress, and depression.

When placed in an environment where overstimulation occurs and the HSP is unable to recoup and recover, they find it more and more challenging to be able to keep everything together. Dr. Aron has always stipulated that HSPs need a time to "pause and reflect" to be able to hit the reset button.

Some HSPs find that the antidote to worry and stress lies in helping others. While this is a fine and noble pursuit, there should be a warning to accompany this choice. As a Highly Sensitive Person, you could become too attached and invested in the person or cause and this could be to your own detriment.

Learning to say "No" for a Highly Sensitive Person can be extremely difficult to do; however, it's better than agreeing to everything and everyone. Remember that as a Highly Sensitive Person, you must have enough time to yourself where you can recharge your batteries and look at resolving your own issues. When you're constantly agreeing to assist everyone else, something's got to give, and it is likely to be you, the HSP.

We live in a world where we are literally overwhelmed by choice. We actually have too much choice, if you come to think about it. Just going to the store to buy milk could prove to be challenging. Do you choose a flavored milk such as coconut or vanilla, 2% or half-and-half? The number of choices available in just a small convenience shopping environment can be totally overwhelming for a Highly Sensitive Person. Limit your exposure to these situations and try and make your decision regarding what you want at home. Write out a shopping list before you leave home. This could provide you with a fair amount of relief once in the store. Stick with the same brands all the time or find someone else to assist you with this menial chore that you know could stress you out.

Two specific processes can create excessive worry for Highly Sensitive Persons; the first is overthinking and the second is ruminating. When we overthink things, we think things through again and again before we come to any conclusion. Ruminating, on the other hand, involves rethinking decisions and replaying them in your mind as though the action is going to have any sort of effect or influence on what has already taken place. Ruminating is a complete waste of time and creates unnecessary amounts of stress, anxiety, and worry.

We worry about things that have happened, that are about to happen, and even those things that might have happened, but didn't. There's no point in wasting valuable energy concerning yourself with theories about what may have been.

You incessantly worry about what people think of you, or what they're likely to think of you. This often includes family members, and you take on the worrier role for everyone.

Stress is an excellent reason for you to worry about everything. Unfortunately, worrying will never provide solutions for problems that you have no control over.

Let's face it, we are surrounded by far too much "stuff." This includes all of our material possessions and clutter that happens to be around us. If we want to regain some control over the things we worry about as HSPs, we need to be prepared to let go of a lot of the things that we've been hanging onto for years. Clutter serves no purpose other than to distract us from those things that we ought to be spending our time focusing on. Cutting back on clutter and learning how to simplify our lives is one of the ways that we can also regain control over our thought processes to eliminate worry.

Overcoming Worry Using Emotional Intelligence

We can easily get into the habit of thinking negatively if we don't learn how to control where our thoughts go. Two ways to avoid this are to practice meditation and mindfulness habits.

If you're not already familiar with the routine of daily meditation then it is worth your adding this to your morning routine. Meditation involves taking some quiet time to be with yourself and your thoughts. It could be spent in spiritual contemplation, drawing closer to God, Allah, or any other higher being that you pay homage to.

Many choose to practice yoga or Tai Chi, to create balance and harmony between their physical side, their emotional side, and their spiritual side. Whatever you choose to do, begin slowly. Even 5-10 minutes each morning can have a positive effect on setting the right tone for the day.

For others, this time could be spent journaling or contemplating deeper questions surrounding life. There are even apps such as Calm and Headspace available that can lead you in a guided morning meditation.

Practicing mindfulness will enable you to shut out much of the busyness that typically goes on within your mind. We process an average of 40,000 to 50,000 different thoughts in a day. Mindfulness can help you to clear away much of the clutter and background noise that take root in our minds daily.

You can practice becoming mindful by first finding an inanimate object such as a glass, or a mug, or even a salt shaker. Mindfulness requires intense focus where all of your attention is directed purely at the object in front of you. Pay attention to its shape and form, its texture, and what it is made of. The purpose of mindfulness is for you to be present in the moment, this moment, and this moment only.

Regarding the issue of sleep, one of the things that can cause an HSP to worry is not getting sufficient sleep and rest. It stands to reason that when you're actually sleeping, your brain cannot be working overtime to solve some impossible task or problem. We understand that HSPs need more sleep than non-sensitive individuals. This is because while you're sleeping, you're able to also rest and recover from any overstimulation that may have taken place during the course of the day. Be sure to get enough hours of sleep every night. Dr. Aron recommends slight changes for those who are self-proclaimed "morning people," versus "evening people." This may mean making a slight change to your daily routine, but if it results in less worry and stress, it will all be worth it.

If you find that you're battling to fall asleep because you have too many thoughts and ideas running through your mind when you should be resting, there are a couple of techniques that you can try to resolve this. You can either curl up with a good book (one that's not going to excite you further), or you can put pen to paper and try to figure out what is preventing you from resting peacefully. Sometimes writing things down can bring clarity to mind and relieve you of the mental fatigue and worry that you're currently experiencing.

Simply being able to close your eyes can make all the difference when it comes to overstimulation. Statistics show that around 80% of all stimulation happens through the eyes, so reducing it can be done by shutting them, even briefly. This is a brilliant habit to get into when it comes to reducing feelings of stress and worry. If you happen to receive too many stimuli when driving in peak traffic, taking a few minutes with your eyes closed once you reach your destination will do wonders to calm any frazzled nerves you may be experiencing. This will also set you up for any challenges that you may need to face at the start of your day.

Worry can come in all shapes and sizes and is often made worse when, as HSPs, we are overly concerned with what others think about us. We may equate this to our being shy or introverted. This is simply not true. Depending on the situation, even the most prominent, extroverted individuals still feel nervous in front of strangers or when addressing people, even if this is just for a short while. Try and remain calm and remind yourself that you are not shy, and you are not an introvert. HSPs are different from introverts. According to Dr. Aron, approximately 40% of all HSPs are actually extroverts, which possibly debunks your theory about being shy. Try to ignore whatever is going through your mind and practice both self- and social-awareness to ignore the voices that are telling you that everyone else is there to judge you. Believe me, you won't be the only one with sweaty palms, feeling anxious about meeting new people. It is a natural response, given any environment or activity that's out of the ordinary.

The intuition of an HSP will constantly have them worrying about the welfare of those around them. The reason for this is that you care so deeply about everyone else. Learning how to let go of this is not as easy as it sounds. This is one of the innate characteristics that HSPs will always have.

Rely on your intuition and the ability to work alongside other team members to stop worrying about whether a task, assignment, or project is good enough to hand in on time. Rather than setting yourself up for failure because you're adamant that everything must be 100% perfect before it can be submitted, accept that the reality is that nothing will ever achieve perfection. No matter how much attention, effort or hours you put into something, chances will be that it was ready for submission five versions ago. You're losing sleep and your sanity over something that you really don't have any control over. Learn to rely on the rest of your team's judgment by using your intuition as well as social awareness skills.

You may be worrying because you are an HSP. From your perspective, you may only see the negatives rather than all of the benefits that you have to offer an organization based on your current set of skills. Depending on the industry that you operate within and your current job description, more often than not, Highly Sensitive Persons are a real asset to the organizations they work for. It is likely though, as an HSP, you cannot see this for yourself. Unless someone has actually pointed this out to you, you may not have accepted that you're excellent in your job. You probably won't believe that your attention to detail can be something that is highly valued by any employer.

Yes, you may be overly sensitive at times, but when your employer and colleagues know this and they can understand this for themselves, then this could all work out in everyone's favor. This is where sharing information is extremely important right from the moment you walk in the door.

One of the biggest challenges for someone who is an HSP is that they do not have a built-in mechanism to be able to self-regulate against the challenges of everyday life. This is hard enough for a non-sensitive person to accomplish. Using emotional intelligence, you need to be able to intuit your own feelings. What's happening with your own emotions? Without this information, you won't be able to deal with the common stresses that can be found each and every day of your life.

You're great at being able to use your intuition to know what others are feeling, but it's understanding when to limit that intuition so that you don't get swallowed up in their emotions at the same time.

Other areas of emotional intelligence that HSPs are really skilled in are empathy and compassion. Once again, to reiterate the point made above, using sound emotional intelligence judgement involves realizing when you're becoming overly invested in the situation and being able to limit your empathy to the point where it's still under your control. Having emotional intelligence means that you can successfully work with each of these situations and emotions, without becoming too involved on a personal level.

Being overloaded with worry can actually affect your mental health in the long run which happens when worrying leads to more serious anxiety, which can lead to panic attacks, which can also then lead to depression. Serious depression can have a devastating effect on your overall health.

If it gets to the stage where you are past the levels of anxiety and panic attacks and you feel yourself heading toward depression, please seek professional help from a certified mental health practitioner. They will be able to assist you with various forms of treatment or exercises that can benefit you. Do not delay in reaching out for assistance if you feel that there has been a major shift in your mood, you want to do nothing more than lie in bed all day, or if you're having thoughts of suicide.

If you are so worried that you're different from everyone else that you actually do call on a medical practitioner and they brush your highly sensitive personality off as just being shy or introverted, then you must advocate for yourself. You may need to explain in your calmest, most rational voice that you are a Highly Sensitive Person and request them to be treating you accordingly. In the event that they aren't the type of practitioner who is open and sensitive to this type of condition then you need to keep on looking for someone who is—believe me, they are out there.

According to Nancy Boyle, from The Village Family Service Center, high emotional intelligence is described in the words "I feel…" Emotions are all demonstrated openly rather than trying to keep them hidden. They aren't obsessed with negative thinking and emotions. They make choices based on the thoughts they have about the situation and common sense, or reasoning. They are confident, determined, positive, thorough, cautious, precise, warm, passionate, and pleasant (Boyle, n.d.).

A lack of emotional intelligence is characterized by saying things like "You constantly lead me to believe…" These people struggle to describe their emotions to others by speaking about them. Depressing feelings take over, making them feel even worse about situations. They act on impulse without thinking about it or basing their choices on logical reasoning. These individuals can be challenging, arrogant, critical, fussy, difficult to please, easy to distract, and egotistical.

Dealing with these emotions should be done using the four-step emotional intelligence process.

Using emotional intelligence, is how you address all the negative emotions associated with worry and anxiety.

Self-Awareness

When you're self-aware, you can name each of the different emotions that you're feeling without allowing them to take control over you. Individuals wanting to improve their self-awareness skills can practice the following techniques:

Speak with those around you with whom you associate with on a regular basis such as loved ones, employers, colleagues, and close friends to ask them to provide you with honest feedback as to how you deal with stress.

You can also look inwards and ask yourself the following questions:

- Are there areas that need to be improved with regard to your emotions?
- Are your decisions influenced by your feelings?

- Do you accept accountability for your decisions and actions?
- Do your emotions influence the way you respond to situations?
- How do your emotions affect the way you treat others?
- How are your coping mechanisms at the moment? What do you do to alleviate worry?
- Is your communication affected?
- What type of emotions are you feeling? Can you name them?

Self-Regulation

Self-regulation is defined as "the ability to control emotions and impulses." If you can control your impulses and emotions, then your moods will seldom fluctuate. You won't become angry or frustrated for no apparent reason. You will be able to regulate your moods to the point where you won't feel totally overwhelmed by them. Self-regulation is an emotional intelligence skill that needs to be learned. It involves learning to pause and reflect before expressing emotion. This requires both time and patience, as well as being prepared to fail at times, allowing each of these failures to teach us valuable lessons in controlling our emotions. Especially as an HSP, you may need to find outlets that will assist you in keeping your emotions under control. Some of these techniques may include the following:

- Keeping physically fit through regular exercise. Choose an exercise that you enjoy doing so that you will be motivated to do it regularly to get the maximum benefit from it.
- Choosing to follow a healthy diet. This will assist you in keeping physically fit, as it takes more than a healthy body to ensure that your mind remains alert and active.
- Become involved with engaging hobbies that stimulate the mind without becoming overwhelming.
- Regular social interaction with friends. Socialize with those who understand what you need as a Highly Sensitive Person. When it's all becoming too much, they will understand when you excuse yourself. Together with your friends who understand you, choose activities that don't cause overwhelm.

Tap into the imaginative side that highly sensitive individuals are known for and create something. This could be through writing, poetry, music, dance, art, or various other outlets that you can use to express yourself. If you're not sure what your preferred form of creative expression is just yet, then try your hand at a number of different activities until you discover what's right for you. The possibilities are endless, from art classes to Zumba lessons, and everything in between.

Another key ingredient when it comes to self-regulation is practicing meditation. This can take on many different forms depending on what is most comfortable for you. Are you comfortable getting in touch with your spiritual side or would you prefer to schedule time for reading motivational material? Some prefer practicing yoga, deep breathing exercises, or using ancient Tibetan bowls.

Self-regulation involves the practice of pausing and reflecting before acting. Remember that you are unable to control everything.

Social Awareness and Management

Practice really listening to others when they are talking to you. This involves much more than simply making eye contact with them. It's watching your own body language to ensure that you're not sending the wrong signals. Social awareness involves developing your relationships with those around you—those you like, as well as those you barely tolerate. Be aware that you may be saying one thing verbally, yet you're telling the person you're communicating with something completely different with your facial expressions and other cues.

There are ways that you can improve these skills, so that they prevent emotional stress:

- Consider the other person's perspective. This will allow you to gain better insight as to why they are behaving as they are. It would be like experiencing them as if you were in their shoes, rather than your own.
- Ask yourself questions regarding those things that you may not be able to see. Why are they responding or reacting in a particular way?
- What are they not saying? Is there something between the lines that you have yet to discover?

Genuine listening means being able to show empathy for the person without judging them for what they are saying. It's more than listening with an intent to respond.

Remember that many times, others simply need someone to listen, and not necessarily to provide a solution for them. They likely already have a solution, but what they really need is empathy and compassion.

CHAPTER 10:
EMOTIONAL OVERLOAD AS AN HSP

"I don't think we should have less information in the world. The information age has yielded great advances in medicine, agriculture, transportation and many other fields. But the problem is twofold. One, we are assaulted with more information than any one of us can handle. Two, beyond the overload, too much information often leads to bad decisions."
~ *Daniel Levitin*

From the time the Highly Sensitive Person is an infant, they are constantly trying to cope with emotional overload. This is often thanks to parents and loved ones who theoretically mean well, but create a greater sensory overload than the infant is able to handle. Constant fussing over an infant by well-meaning caregivers can be the cause of a sensory onslaught that works against the needs of the child, rather than with them.

Emotional Overload as an HSP

Some of the ways that highly sensitive individuals become emotionally overwhelmed and overloaded is by taking on the emotions of everyone around them. Toward the beginning of this book, we discussed that they are like sponges that are constantly absorbing whatever is happening around them. If you compared this with a glass that someone was pouring liquid into, the glass will have reached its maximum capacity when it was full. What happened with anything after that point was wasted. Unfortunately for the HSP, they don't have an "off" switch, or a means of indicating when their glass is full, other than feelings of having to escape to be on their own.

The escapism is not specifically directed at anyone or due to anything specific (even though some people are keen to jump to that conclusion). It is simply that the HSP cannot absorb anything more. They are emotionally full and need time on their own, or with someone who understands them fully, to be able to unwind and get to the point where they can once again begin taking on the energy that those around them are discharging.

HSPs aren't only absorbing whatever is communicated verbally. They're absorbing all the raw emotion that goes along with it. Some of this emotion can only be felt if you're paying particular attention to what is happening around you. It's no wonder that HSPs are often emotionally exhausted. The only solution to this scenario is for them to make a break for it where solitude is the antidote to overstimulation. HSPs need a lot more rest than those who are not highly sensitive or invested in the situation. It's best for them to spend this time on their own where they can restore their emotional equilibrium. There's no specific timeframe as to how long the HSP will need to recover from overstimulation. This depends on two things—how overstimulated they are and the different techniques that they use to relax and unwind.

For some, unwinding means retreating to a solitary place where it's just them, their thoughts, and possibly some gentle, relaxing music or a good book. What's necessary to help the unwinding process is unique and specific to everyone. It may be a long, relaxing bath by candlelight with a few drops of invigorating or soothing essential oil. Whatever it is, be sure to take however much time is necessary to return to a normal level.

Some other things that specifically overload your sensory perception are loud noises and sudden sounds that you weren't anticipating. These overstimulate any Highly Sensitive Person causing them to become startled to the point where they feel that they are no longer in control of their emotions. If this is excessive, it may even lead to panic attacks. For this reason, it's extremely important that the HSP is able to unwind and offload the emotions as quickly as possible. Since most of the stimulation happens through hearing—simply finding a quiet place where you can close your eyes for a few minutes could potentially be all that you need to kick start your ability to take on further stimuli.

Being overstimulated is a condition that nobody really asks for or wants. If you don't like too many things going on around you, all vying for your attention as a non-HSP, imagine what this feels like for an HSP? They experience all of this a hundred-fold more than could ever be experienced by someone who's a non-HSP. The ability to sense and feel the emotions of everything and everyone can be emotionally draining for the HSP.

An HSP does not perform well under pressure, especially when this relates to tasks that need to complete within a certain amount of time. Consider the pressure that they must feel each time that they face exams or assessments that are against the clock. For the Highly Sensitive Person, the clock represents yet another challenge in an already tense environment. As adults, even working with something as basic as a "To Do List" can create an insane amount of pressure, especially if they never manage to work through it to completion within the self-imposed timelines. Notice how I've identified that they have potentially placed the limitation on themselves? Even this is too much for them and they can end up extremely stressed.

That beautiful, glorious brain of the Highly Sensitive Person is constantly searching for answers and digging deeper than their non-sensitive counterparts. This will naturally result in thinking and contemplating on things like the meaning of life. The HSP insists on finding meaning everywhere, in every conversation, in every interaction, in everything they observe around them. It's no wonder that they need a lot more rest and relaxation by the end of the day after experiencing something that can be so physically and mentally taxing on the system.

Mysteries interest and excite you. I'm not referring to curling up and reading Sir Arthur Conan Doyle's *Sherlock Holmes*, or other mystery novels. The mysteries that I'm referring to are some of the greatest mysteries of the universe. These questions burn deep within the heart and soul of an HSP and demand genuine answers. They find it strange that their non-HSP counterparts aren't as interested in discovering major answers to the inner workings of the universe.

You need to be able to identify each of the things that causes you emotional overload. We already know that, for a non-HSP, there are some major life changes that automatically bring about stress and challenges, even for them. One such thing is having to undergo a major change. This could be anything from changing jobs to relocating. Moving to a new house (even within the same city) can prove to be overstimulating because you're having to re-create your safe space all over again.

Changing jobs, coming into a totally new environment where there are different people, a new way of working, and even different operating systems can leave an HSP feeling completely frazzled by the end of the day, let alone overwhelmed. Changes in personal relationships, having to face a break-up or divorce, or losing a loved one are all major stressors for the HSP, and they will need a strong support system as well as a lot of down time or quiet time where they can be alone to process the millions of thoughts and emotions that seem to be attacking them from every angle all at once. HSPs don't handle change well at all. That's why for them, one of the most crucial things is for them to have stability in their lives.

Even changes with friends, or something as simple as missing the day that the garbage is collected can throw them completely off kilter. Most of their lives have been formed and developed around strong, reliable routines. This is what manages to keep them secure and grounded. Potential changes to these routines that they have grown to rely on are always possible. Sure, there will always be certain things that you have no control over, and you cannot hope to keep the same no matter how hard you try. These are things such as the weather, the economy, and losing loved ones. People don't always die of old age. Life is a path that we all need to walk, but it's challenging for an HSP to accept such major changes to their lives, especially when they are particularly close to someone who has died.

Vacationing with friends or family can prove to be overwhelming, especially when it's somewhere that you've never been before—even traveling to this destination can have alarm bells ringing if you're flying and you've never been on an airplane before. This is potentially the height of overstimulation for any HSP, to be stuck on an airplane with literally hundreds of people, all talking, coughing, sneezing, snoring, watching movies, attendants walking up and down the aisles, and people digging in and out of overhead luggage. All of this could prove too much for you to try to deal with, within a confined space. One of the best tactics to use for dealing with all this overstimulation would be to close your eyes, trying to block out as much of what is going on around you as possible, putting some headphones on, and playing some of your best music that helps you to restore your peace and calm. Another thing would be to focus on your breathing by inhaling deeply all the way down into your diaphragm, allowing the air to flow through your body, calming the mind. Breathe out through the mouth slowly until you know that all the breath is completely expelled. Repeat this process a couple of times more until you can feel yourself beginning to relax.

You may wish to remain like this until most of the passengers are sleeping (especially if you happen to be on a long flight). When the majority of the passengers are sleeping, you will discover that the overstimulation is not as great as it was earlier. This may be a good time for you to do the things that you would have normally done if you were alone. Sit back and read, or watch an inflight movie, catch up on some travel blogs, and just enjoy the peace and quiet that has enveloped the passenger deck of the aircraft. Prepare yourself for the major stimulation that's going to take place at the instant that the flight lands.

As an HSP, one useful tip for aircraft travel would be to choose a window seat. In that way, you won't have the challenge of getting up and moving whenever one of the passengers needs something from the overhead bins, or they need to use the onboard toilets. You can also do your best to get to the front of the line, so that you will be one of the first to board the aircraft. Once your flight lands, wait until almost all of the passengers have left the plane before you think about moving. This will assist you in more than one way:

1. Firstly, you will not have to fight your way to access your carry-on luggage in the overhead bins because, by the time you are ready to do so, the flight will be just about empty. If you need assistance, there will still be flight attendants onboard.

2. Secondly, you won't need to line up to disembark the flight. Once again, most of the passengers would have stormed the exits to get off of the flight first.
3. Thirdly, the conveyor belt area to where all of the bags are transported would have also become a lot less crowded. This would result in your bags being on the conveyor without hundreds of other bags. You will be able to simply collect your bags and be on your way, with minimal fuss and without the massive onslaught of all the passengers from the same flight.

Airports, train stations, bus terminals, and subway stations can be completely overwhelming for any HSP because of all of the different types of stimuli experienced. You are dealing with extreme sounds, crowds of people, odors, bright lights, the constant noise of overhead messages being broadcasted, billboards that are ever-changing with travel information, and the constant drone of hundreds, if not thousands, of people rushing to get to where they want to be.

The HSP would probably, by this point, need to find a really quiet space where they can simply unwind, without having to deal with more stimulus than they really need to. When travelling, especially to destinations with which you are unfamiliar, each of these challenges needs to be taken into consideration if there happens to be an HSP or be with someone who is one. Being as prepared as possible with soothing sounds, music, a good book, comfortable clothing, and somewhere quiet to unwind should definitely be a part of your itinerary. Your ultimate destination can also not be anywhere that they will feel even more overwhelmed. Remember that they need to be able to recover from all of the excess stimulation that they've taken on.

Once you finally arrive at your destination, allow the HSP however long they need to recover from whatever form of travel you took to get there. Even if this means that you give them a day of solitude to get over jet lag and the stimulation that came with it, they may want to just spend their day in their room with the curtains drawn, self-soothing with calming music, or resting in order for them to be able to function through the remainder of their vacation.

There are many things that may cause HSPs to be over-stimulated. This could be anything from hunger pangs to their inability to deal with stimulation from coffee, energy drinks or alcohol. You will seldom find an HSP who has the capacity to party all night without paying a hefty price for it in the days that follow. This is not to say that all HSPs are introverted and need their own space. We have already mentioned that of all HSPs—up to 40% of them—are extroverts, which means that they won't have any trouble partying along with you. It may just mean that they do it without having to load up on caffeine or alcohol first.

How Does it Feel to be Overstimulated?

There are many ways that overstimulation can manifest in an individual. This can present as physical and emotional feelings, creating a sense of inner restlessness, as indicated by Tom Falkenstein, author of *The Highly Sensitive Man*. Any or all of these feelings and emotions, if not dealt with, can ultimately result in exhaustion because the nervous system is permanently on overdrive. If we consider the example above, it is impossible to prevent overstimulation. You cannot prevent being stimulated by things going on around you. It's impossible for this to be accomplished.

You cannot foresee or prevent any eventuality. Some of the examples that Falkenstein gives are pretty straightforward, ordinary day-to-day examples such as visiting the local market or store, having to give a presentation at work, and being in a crowded place during a commute. What we need to be acutely aware of, however, is that chronic overstimulation is possible. This can occur when your nervous system doesn't have the ability to pause and reset, or where there are no breaks that would allow you to relax and recharge. This results in the HSP becoming tense due to overstimulation, and because they are constantly facing a variety of stimuli, emotions continue to run at full throttle.

Falkenstein goes on to warn what could happen if you're not able to unwind—serious health problems could occur, particularly when it comes to mental health. This is where being able to regulate your emotions and your feelings becomes extremely important, so that your system is able to remain healthy and functioning at its best.

He provides several potential solutions when it comes to working with overstimulation. Some of these are as follows:

- Using your imagination to recall ways that have helped you to overcome overstimulation previously. Whenever you discover something that's successful, make a note of what you did so that you can choose to repeat it whenever you're feeling overwhelmed. Who was with you when you successfully managed to get your emotions under control?

- We always have freedom of choice when it comes to dealing with our emotions. We can choose how we manage overstimulation. We may make use of breathing exercises or meditation, mindfulness, or music. Finding the right solution for the emotions you happen to be dealing with at any one time may require sufficient practice to get the feelings of overstimulation back under control. Sometimes these choices lead us to changing the way we behave. In the previous example regarding flight travel, simply by delaying your actions you are able to eliminate a lot of the stimulation that you may have been feeling. Changing behavior necessitates making a conscious decision. It's the ability to think things through for yourself to come up with alternative solutions that are going to be right for you and will bring you peace, rather than stress and anxiety.

- Self-soothing or self-care can be a great way to discover those things that could potentially help you to overcome where you are at the moment, to a place that's better suited to how you feel. This is accomplished by showing yourself empathy and compassion (Falkenstein, 2019).

Julie Bjelland shares the way that some HSPs feel when they are emotionally overstimulated.

- For some, it's as though they're trapped in a building that's on fire and cannot escape.
- The constant attack of every single sensation all at once. This creates a knock-on effect of wanting to escape to somewhere that's peaceful where they can be on their own to deal with stressors and triggers.
- For others, it feels like electricity, or an experience where they're not even a part of it—they feel like they're observing the scene from overhead, rather than being in control.
- Feelings of being totally overwhelmed by emotions all at once where they're unable to do anything about it.

- For almost every one of her descriptions, each identified the need to be able to escape to an environment where there was peace and calm, and where they could feel safe.

Conventional Ways of Overcoming Overwhelm

We've already spoken about music as an antidote to overwhelm. Make a specific playlist of songs that have the capacity to restore your equilibrium. Carry your headphones around with you. This could offer an immediate solution no matter where you are, as you can simply put your headphones on and allow the music to transport you to a calm and peaceful place. There are many apps available online that offer soothing and relaxing music. Download several of these and put together a playlist that's going to restore your calm.

Find someplace quiet where you can be alone with your thoughts. This doesn't always need to be a place where you are isolated and alone. Consider areas where you can still be a part of society, but where there's very limited noise. Some of these places include libraries and museums. You may even be able to find a reasonably quiet bookstore, or a place that allows you to read while you're there. This environment needs to be accessible as quickly as possible. I would make a list of various go-to safe spaces where you're able to restore peace and calm to your life.

If you are an HSP and happen to be facing overwhelm and overstimulation in any sphere of your life, you're already quite aware of the impact that it can have on your system. Some of what we've been discussing would cause a certain amount of stress in anyone's life. For the HSP though, in order to move past the amount of stress caused, they would probably need a significant amount of time to unwind.

These go-to quiet places mentioned above could potentially be any nearby place that's quiet. HSPs need to actively work at this self-soothing process in order to be able to get over hyper-stimulation and overwhelm.

Another way to get away from it all in order to unwind is by unplugging from all forms of social media for a set amount of time. There are several ways of doing this that can be effective. Simply switching off for a particular amount of time is one idea. Setting it aside in another room and making your way outside into the fresh air without it is another. Social media can attack your senses and add to the amount of stimulation you're already trying to deal with.

Have you tried to make friends with others who are exactly like you? They can appreciate your situation and what you're going through because they understand and accept you for who you are. They experience exactly the same types of overstimulation as you're trying to process. They're not going to take exception if you tell them that you need some "alone" or "quiet" time.

Overcoming Emotional Overload Using Emotional Intelligence

Once again, the starting point for overcoming overstimulation and making use of emotional intelligence needs to begin with identifying the emotions you're feeling. This process can be relatively simple and straightforward when you're working through your emotions. For a Highly Sensitive Person, this is one of the characteristics of emotional intelligence that they excel at. Because everything about being an HSP is linked to emotions and feelings, if you battle identifying how you are feeling then you may need to become grounded and get back in touch with your feelings in that particular moment.

If you feel overwhelmed by too many emotions and are feeling as though they are being directed at you from every direction, stop, pause, and reflect on your feelings. Name the emotion(s) you are experiencing at the time. This involves being specific about what you're feeling, what you're thinking, what you're allowing others to see, and what vibe you are giving off. Are you prepared to accept responsibility and accountability for the way that you are feeling? This is directly linked to self-awareness.

As an HSP, you have the advantage of being able to recognize and appreciate varying points of view when it comes to dealing with emotions. You can pick up both negative and positive emotions. While we all want to be feeling what's good and what makes us feel happy, we need to be just as realistic that the opposite is just as important. For us to be able to appreciate those times when positive events occur, causing us to feel joy, peace, and contentment, we need to have experienced sadness, pain, failure, and anxiety. We need to be realistic. We cannot survive and thrive in an emotional vacuum where we limit our emotions to only positive ones. We need to admit to ourselves and others when we aren't doing well and when we're feeling overwhelmed by everything going on around us. There's no point in forcing these emotions down and pretending that everything is fine. Just as much as you need an outlet to self-soothe, you also need to be able to express yourself when you're not coping.

Some of the ways that you can add to your self-awareness model is by considering how others are currently seeing you. What are your current strengths and weaknesses? This is a worthwhile exercise used to determine whether you're currently allowing all of the emotions around you to negatively influence you, or whether you've been able to recover sufficiently. Don't berate yourself or keep beating yourself over the head about those times when you're not actually doing as well. This happens with everyone. It would be completely unnatural for you to be functioning at full speed, and in happy mode consistently. It's impossible, even for the most highly skilled, or someone with extremely high emotional intelligence. We all have "down days" and times when we know that we're really not at our best.

As an HSP, be prepared to trust what your intuition is telling you. Intuition is one of your key qualities. Your subconscious is in control when it comes to your intuition. If your gut is telling you that something isn't quite right with a person or a situation, you should know by now that you need to be trusting these feelings because they're always telling you something of importance.

One way that you could keep a track record of these "moods" and potential "swings" is by keeping a journal where you write what has taken place throughout the day, how you dealt it, and also whether there were things that you could have done differently. This allows you to look at yourself objectively and from a point of emotional intelligence. Keeping a journal allows you to track specific changes that you'd like to see in your life, especially something like making use of EQ to overcome some of the more common challenges that you have to deal with. Journaling has always been seen as a means of therapeutic intervention.

You may decide to purchase a paper journal that you can make notes in at the end of each day, or perhaps you would prefer to journal digitally on your tablet or laptop. There are several important concepts to consider when you choose to journal. Journaling is a deeply personal and private activity. It's up to you who you decide to share it with—or not. If you're not entirely comfortable sharing your writing, then keep it for your eyes only. Understand that allowing others access to your journals could defeat the object of it being a special, private, safe space where you can express yourself freely without having anyone judge you or your beliefs. You should be free to vent or express all of your emotions deeply and freely on the pages.

What really motivates you and keeps you wanting to get up in the morning and move forward? Is it success, or the achievement of certain goals, or perhaps you have a desire to make someone proud of you. Understanding your key motivation will help you to continue toward the achievement of your goals.

When it comes to self-management and becoming overstimulated, you have the capacity to know yourself and your emotions better than anyone else. If you're aware that a particular place, person, or situation has the potential to get the better of you, then it's up to you to do your best to avoid the situation for your own protection. Self-awareness will allow you to identify what sets you off or makes you feel overstimulated and do something about it.

In the example given earlier regarding the vacation, there were some excellent self-awareness coping mechanisms used to shut out a lot of the external stimuli; closing your eyes, putting your headphones on, and letting calming beats do their thing to reduce the levels of stress and anxiety. Also discussed was relocating to a library, bookstore, museum, or even a quiet coffee shop or café to enjoy a book or relaxing moments with headphones on.

Another technique used to preempt overwhelm is scheduling. If you don't have a specific schedule, put one together and then do your best to stick to it. This will provide structure in your life which is part of self-awareness. When your schedule gets off track, you will probably begin to feel out of control. Double-check where you're meant to be, what you're supposed to be doing, and get back on track as quickly as possible. It's understood that life happens and occasionally, there are events or situations that are completely out of our control. Instead of allowing these things to paralyze us in the moment because we weren't prepared to face them, stop and figure it out by centering and grounding yourself again through the deep-breathing techniques discussed in previous chapters. To do this, breathe in deeply through your nose, filling your lungs to capacity so that your stomach is tight. Release the breath through your mouth by blowing gently until all the oxygen has been expelled from your lungs. Repeat this process several times until you feel as though you are back in control of your emotions.

It is especially important to control your emotions when it comes to getting angry. It's perfectly understandable that you may be angry on occasion. The key is to express your anger in a healthy manner, directed appropriately. Also, remember that there's a big difference between being overwhelmed and being angry. This is one of the main reasons that the very first thing you should be mastering in emotional intelligence is being able to give your emotions names. You need to be able to identify when you are angry, or jealous, or frustrated, or overwhelmed, just as you need to be able to identify when you're feeling relaxed, happy, content, and confident.

Chapter 11: HSP Relationships Using Emotional Intelligence

"As a highly sensitive person, I can sense your mood from a mile away. Don't try to hide it. You're not fooling me."
~ Tracy M. Kusmierz

Hsps and Relationships

One of the most under-researched elements when it comes to Highly Sensitive Persons is the relationships that they have with others. I'm not referring to platonic relationships or associations with those you work or come into contact with on a daily basis. I am referring to long-term, loving relationships and genuine connections with others in the world. Connecting with others in a meaningful way is an emotional intelligence skill. For the HSP, they connect on an emotional level and can intuit everything. Is it possible that if HSPs were known and understood better that they could potentially be more successful in relationships?

This is not to say that they aren't successful to a degree; however, Dr. Aron's studies claim that approximately 34% of intimate relationships involve at least one HSP. For the Highly Sensitive Person, they often feel frustrated with the relationship because they feel as though their needs aren't being met. Most of this is because they feel as though they are being misunderstood. If they're in a relationship with a non-HSP, they can often be labelled as being too sensitive, too emotional, and are often told to "get over their issues." Lack of understanding of HSPs is potentially the number one reason for these relationships failing. Stop feeling sorry for yourself and embrace yourself as being different from the rest of the world (well, apart from the other 15% to 20%).

Here are just some of the benefits of being in a relationship with an HSP:

- They're going to love you more deeply than anyone else ever will. All of their emotions are heightened, so expect a bit of an emotional rollercoaster as they meet your friends and as you go out. They will be able to survey an environment long before you've even settled in. Trust them if they ask to go somewhere else, as they will be right to do so. Allow them to trust their instincts and learn to appreciate this about them.

- Get used to them being emotional at both extremes. If you don't do all that "emotional stuff," then call it quits right away. They're clearly not for you. HSPs can move from shrieks of laughter deep within their souls, to sobbing uncontrollably during sad parts of a movie. As long as you provide them with a shoulder to lean on and a box of Kleenex, you'll be fine.

There are a couple of things you should avoid:

- Don't judge them for the empathy they display toward others. You may well need to be on the receiving end of that empathy and compassion at some stage and theirs is a unique gift in that they can sense exactly what it is that you need, and when you need it. You may not be able to understand it at the beginning of your relationship, but know that whatever you need them for and whenever, they will be there for you unconditionally and without question. They are someone who will always have your back.

- Highly Sensitive Persons are easily overwhelmed. Chapter 10 has been exclusively dedicated to this. From a relationship perspective, understand that they need some alone time, or down time where they have the opportunity to simply return to a state of normality. Don't rush them, even if you originally had plans, as this could only serve to escalate the situation further. Give them both time and space and they will surprise you by recovering in time for your plans because one of the last things that HSPs want to do is disappoint. Be considerate about their self-care routine. You may even be able to assist them by running a bath or playing some soothing music. They may need their own space where they can be for a while to unwind sufficiently after even one of the most normal days at the office. The stress and overstimulation of the workplace followed by traffic could increase the levels of anxiety that your partner is feeling. They need to be able to release and restore a level of normality.

- We've discussed how HSPs possess an enhanced sense of smell. They can be overwhelmed by certain smells which they have the ability to pick up long before anyone else. Some of these scents may irritate them. As an example, I'm particularly sensitive to anything that has musk in it. It makes me physically ill. How do you explain to someone that you have an ultra-sensitive nose and the perfume, deodorant, or after shave that they're wearing is making you physically ill? Because I am sensitive to how others feel, I can never be straightforward and honest about this. I do the next best thing, and that's to remove myself from the environment with the offending smell. This can be done in a sensitive way as well, so feelings are not hurt.

If you happen to be in a relationship with an HSP, start off by asking them if there are any particular olfactory sensitivities they have, or scents that they prefer. Just as much as not liking a particular fragrance, they may absolutely adore another one. The right way of working around this sensitivity is by coming to a mutually-beneficial agreement that works for both of you.

HSPs and Emotions in Relationships

We've explained that Highly Sensitive Persons feel things on a much deeper level than those who are non-HSPs.

This allows them to connect more deeply than you could ever imagine. They love more deeply, they are more passionate, and as a matter of fact, all of their senses are consistently heightened. So, how do you deal with someone who is always on edge when it comes to emotions? They can experience the highest of highs and the lowest of lows within a very short time range. This is because they feel so deeply. A book or movie that's captured their attention can keep them fully engrossed with their box of Kleenex, or they can become totally emotionally invested as each scene is revealed. Whatever you do, don't expect them to watch violent or horror movies where there is a lot of blood and gore because this upsets them too much. Consider that they actually see themselves in each of the characters of the films that they see, and this might explain why they can become overly emotional while watching.

They participate in the entire experience, so be prepared to provide them with support as they may require.

As long as you're romantically involved with a Highly Sensitive Person, they will likely know when you need some extra love and nurturing before you do. They can pick up the atmosphere from the moment they enter a space. In the same light, don't take them home to meet your folks if there happens to be a major family feud going on. They're going to sense it and it will make them rather uncomfortable.

Your highly sensitive significant other will pick up on the emotions of your other friends and associates as well, so be prepared for some in-depth discussions where they tell you all about what they have sensed just from being around them.

Remember that they are highly empathetic and will always be there to support you in any situation. If you're having a hard time, you can always count on them. One of the few times that they may not necessarily support you though, is if you're highly sociable and you need to be out partying all of the time. For the HSP, the occasional party and get-together is manageable, but to do so constantly doesn't work for them because of the sensory overload and mass stimulation.

Be prepared for them to tell you something that they overheard during a group conversation that you were totally oblivious to. HSPs have acute hearing skills that make them prone to picking up even the smallest of sounds that you wouldn't pay attention to. Some of these things include background noise that's distracting them and preventing them from being fully focused on their work.

Other noises that could possibly irritate the HSP are things like chewing loudly, somebody fidgeting, pen tapping, or someone bouncing their knee in anticipation. Each of these represents stimulation overload for our HSPs and they need to be able to take a break to regroup themselves as often as necessary. This is definitely where a local bookstore or library could come in handy. A few minutes of peace and calm offers a world of good for anyone who is dealing with emotional overload.

These are all situations that you can potentially control by escaping from them. What happens in those instances where you simply cannot remove yourself? Think about your neighborhood where there's a dog that barks nonstop at its own shadow night and day, or your neighbor who has just given birth to a baby and for the first couple of weeks, you are woken by the baby's cries at all hours of the night and early morning. As much as superior hearing can be a huge advantage to, it can also be frustrating for never being able to switch it off.

Something that your partner will appreciate is the pleasure of music that speaks to their senses. As much as they dislike loud and irritating noises, they love to hear music that has been professionally crafted for their listening pleasure.

Other heightened senses that can prove to be challenging in a long-term relationship are things like being extremely sensitive to touch, different types of foods, odors, and pain. They're sensitive to things that people say and do to them. The good news is, however, that if you're in a relationship with an HSP, they love with such a deep and lasting passion (Petsinis, 2019).

For individuals who don't know that they're highly sensitive, relationships can prove to be both challenging and extremely exhausting. They find themselves giving their relationship absolutely everything they have and still failing miserably, often wondering why they are so mentally drained and physically exhausted at the end of the day.

The things that non-HSP people take for granted in a relationship can be extremely demanding for Highly Sensitive Persons. For HSPs, the demands of living life with a home, a spouse, children, and a job, keeping all the plates spinning in the air at the same time can be too much. There are many relationships that simply cannot survive under this type of emotional pressure. It's often too overwhelming for them to handle.

Imagine this type of pressure multiplied. Remember that 34% of all relationships contain at least one HSP. What about relationships where there happen to be two HSPs, where you have two individuals who are constantly picking up each other's emotions? If they've never heard of Highly Sensitive Persons or they don't understand why they're constantly so emotional, or why they pick up on everything, and why they're overstimulated all the time, it can be very challenging. These couples don't know that they each need to schedule alone time, or at least downtime together if there are two HSPs in the relationship.

This is exactly what happened to Hannah Brooks in her first marriage. At the time, she had no idea that she was a Highly Sensitive Person. She'd never even heard the term.

All that she knew was that her marriage was going through some really great times which were fantastic, but when they hit the bad times, they were really tough. She explains that she kept on asking herself what was wrong with her, and why she was constantly feeling totally and utterly overwhelmed all the time. Little did she realize at the time, but her husband was feeling exactly the same way. Here, there were two Highly Sensitive Persons who really loved each other, but never understood what was pushing their buttons, why they were getting so overexcited about it, and how to unwind, relax and recharge to face the next challenge. She wasn't surprised that their marriage didn't last, despite them being very much in love.

Remember, that for an HSP to commit to an individual or a relationship, they're all in and it really is going to take a lot for a marriage to fail, especially when both parties really love each other and are committed for the long haul.

HSPs and Non-Sensitives

Drs. Aron, as in Elaine Aron and Art Aron, the wonderful research psychologists who are ultimately responsible for all of the work that has been done and continues to be done on HSPs, are a typical example of a marriage where there's only one HSP in the equation. In her book, *The Highly Sensitive Person in Love: Understanding and Managing Relationships When the World Overwhelms You*, Dr. Aron describes the relationship that she and her husband have as one that involves a lot of understanding and support. One of the examples she provides sets the tone perfectly. She freely admits that Art loves being the center of attention whenever they're away at conferences. On the other hand, she prefers to sit and talk to someone who appears to be alone and that conversation takes place on a deep level.

Art enjoys waking up early, and going to breakfast and all of the various conference talks and different sessions during the day. He's then also ready to party late into the night with the delegates, making the most of their time away. This is not at the cost of his wife's happiness. It's purely that he understands that none of these things are important to her. She is able to work within the section of the conference where she and her husband are participating. She may even be able to make it down for a few of the meals, but then she needs to be on her own once again because everything has been too much for her, especially with all of the people.

Her husband understands this and supports her in it 100%. Often in the afternoons, she prefers to take long walks outside and you will find them both hand in hand because it is a pastime that they both enjoy. Plus, it gives them precious time to be together. They are used to walking together every evening while at home and Art will tell you that there's nowhere else he would rather be than hand in hand with his wife enjoying the beauty of nature.

They have come to a mutual agreement on what needs to happen whenever she needs to have alone time or to be on her own with her overactive, highly stimulated thoughts. He respects her for that and gives her the space that she needs because he understands her as a Highly Sensitive Person.

Getting back to Hannah, although she was looking inwards to find what was broken and what was wrong with her so that she could try and fix her marriage, the truth is that there was nothing wrong with her at all. She wasn't broken and there was nothing to fix. As a Highly Sensitive Person, her needs were and are unique. They are not the same as the needs of a non-sensitive person. It doesn't help to tell her to "be strong, and fight the good fight," or that "all marriages can be tough, and you need to be able to push through the hard times." Some of these remarks can actually do a Highly Sensitive Person more harm than good. You need to appreciate that an HSP is not suddenly able to change overnight. They cannot "toughen up" and "move on." An HSP is wired completely differently and it would be totally unreasonable for you to expect them to behave in a way that's actually contrary to their innate nature.

It was only after she learned about her sensitivities to everything that Hannah actually began to change her life. She now appreciates her qualities and characteristics as blessings, rather than something that she wished she never had. She confirms that her relationships with those around her are deeply rewarding. Hannah has since remarried and she spends her time working with other HSPs in an attempt to help them to understand some of the emotions that they may be feeling about themselves. According to her, being an HSP could either help or hinder relationships with others in the following ways:

One of the things that we've discussed is that HSPs are extremely good at is picking up the emotional state of others. They're extremely sensitive to the needs of others and will do their very best to attend to those needs as much as they possibly can. In return, they often expect the same kind of treatment from those around them. When this doesn't happen, this can lead to the HSP feeling as though they're not good enough, or that they've done something to offend you because you're not being attentive. There will always be hundreds of different scenarios running through the heads of Highly Sensitive Persons—most of them untrue naturally. However, this is the way that their minds work and this is how they expect you to be able to work with them as well.

Because you pick up things much quicker, or often see things of which most people are blissfully unaware, you can spot characteristics in your partner that are incredible gifts that need to be nurtured. For an HSP, this means being able to build on your natural gifts and skills to further bless the lives of others. Unfortunately, your ability to think things through thoroughly and deeply could prove to be problematic in your relationship. You may actually unnecessarily worry about things that aren't there because you think so deeply. You could be overthinking things instead of trying to use logical reasoning. HSPs are known for ruminating over things that have happened in the past.

Dealing with feelings, which happens to be a self-awareness trait in emotional intelligence, can help you to show your partner how compassionate or empathetic you can be toward them. However, this could also lead you to taking their emotions on as your own. Where the danger comes in is if they're often in a bad mood, or anxious about things. This has the potential to wreak havoc on your health and your own moods.

You may find that your partner is exceptionally loud and noisy. They may enjoy watching sports with the TV volume on high, or the volume of the music in their car may bother you. This is certainly going to be a major problem for you as a Highly Sensitive Person. You will need to make a point of discussing this with them and explaining the effect that all the overstimulation has on you as a Highly Sensitive Person. The next best thing is to decide whether you can live in this type of environment in the long term. Is someone prepared to make some sacrifices for the sake of the relationship?

It can be extremely difficult for HSPs to feel good about themselves. They're constantly imagining that they fall short in everything they do. Naturally, this is not the case; however, they believe in perfection and anything less is simply not good enough. When you're in a relationship with a Highly Sensitive Person and this is how they're feeling, it's going to take a lot of nurturing, comforting, and reassurance that they are not a failure, or you may need to explain that we all fail at times in our lives. Be particularly sensitive to their needs at this time because HSPs are harder on themselves than they are on those around them. Their expectations of themselves set an almost impossible standard for anyone to attain.

During the course of caring for the needs of their partner, an HSP can often lose themselves while trying to be everything to everyone. This could easily lead to them feeling depleted of all of their own energy and reserves, taking them a much longer time for them to be able to recover. Highly Sensitive Persons must be given the chance to spend time unwinding on their own, or they are most likely headed toward their own meltdowns.

Through the use of emotional intelligence techniques of self-awareness and self-management, it's possible for you to operate from a position of strength. This means that you are well-balanced and grounded in your outlook toward others. You can use exactly the same techniques that we've discussed in the previous chapters to be able to utilize each of the positive personality traits that make you who you are as an HSP. Some of these traits are your intuition, your ability to sense emotions deeply, and often long before others know what's happening. As long as you can learn how to name each of these emotions and keep them under control through self-management techniques, you can actively use them to your and your partner's benefit in the relationship.

Don't be afraid to clarify any situations that may seem unclear. It's better to communicate effectively than to be embroiled in an emotional mess because you've misread a situation, or you think that you know what another person is thinking. Social awareness is at play where you function at your best because of your ability to interact with others. When you do interact with others, do your best to avoid taking on all of their emotions. Such transference could be occurring on a subconscious level. The other person is often not even aware of how deeply you will sense their emotions. If you feel that you need to offer compassion or empathy to the person who's emotional state you are taking on, try to open the lines of communication and explain this to them first. Non-sensitive people can be taken aback by the fact that you can sense so much of what they're experiencing. Play this cool, however, because you must avoid taking too many emotions on. As an HSP, you are the one who is able to feel these emotions, along with the individuals experiencing them at the time.

Whenever you feel that it's all becoming too much for you, practice the self-soothing techniques that we've discussed by removing yourself from the situation so that you can breathe, pause, reflect, restore, and recover your own sense of peace, calm, and tranquility before attempting to jump back in to save the day. As an HSP, this is one of your greatest strengths—to be able to restore peace and calm in any given situation.

Conclusion

"We define emotional intelligence as the subset of social intelligence that involves the ability to monitor one's own and others' feelings and emotions, to discriminate among them and to use this information to guide one's thinking and actions."
~ Salovey and Mayer

There has been much said on the different personality traits of an individual who is part of the one-fifth of the population born with the unique characteristics of being a Highly Sensitive Person. It's worth remembering that they are wired differently. It is not as simple as having a behavior that they learned, allowing them to unlearn it. This is an actual innate personality trait that they are born with. They cannot just "get over it," or "learn to shut it down."

People can be very cruel toward others who they don't understand and unfortunately, HSPs can be on the short end of this behavior. Hopefully, there has been at least one thing in the chapters above that has made you sit up and take note of all the gifts, talents, and natural abilities that these individuals bring to the world. If you are an HSP, learn to be kinder to yourself, rather than demanding that you are constantly perfect. Remember that you are going to always be sensitive to the emotions of those around you, no matter what the environment. Always plan some form of escape route, so that you can shut out as much of the stimuli that's coming at you from every angle in a world that is full to the brim with things that could cause overwhelm.

Your escape route needs to make you feel safe, wherever you may be. It is possible to be in a crowded environment without being a part of the crowded environment. I think of a daily commute to the office where you may need to take a bus or a train. If this proves to be too much for you, you may need to look for alternatives, even if they are more taxing on your resources, as they will be better for you when it comes to your sanity.

When it comes to the skills and abilities needed to practice healthy and solid emotional intelligence skills, as an HSP, you already possess many of the required skills and abilities as they pertain to self-awareness and social awareness. Once you can identify your own emotions, where they are coming from, and how to control them effectively, you can learn to manage them better. As an HSP, you need to remember that learning to master emotional intelligence skills is something that takes time, effort, and a lot of practice. There will be times when you will fail, so be kind to yourself whenever this happens because everyone fails at some point. None of us are perfect in every area of our lives.

You are a master at sensing the emotions of others and doing your best to help make things better through compassion and empathy. These are two extremely important EQ skills that many find challenging to master because they're usually so wrapped up in their own world, that they fail to notice what's going on around them. This is where the beautiful Highly Sensitive Persons bring their unique gifts and talents to the world. Because they are able to sense things so deeply and can pick up whenever someone is feeling down or lonely or sad or anxious, they are the ones who make use of their own internal emotional intelligence to sense the pain or discomfort that those around them are experiencing.

Remember to be aware that you could potentially be sucked into the vacuum of emotions that is going on around you. Finely tune those coping mechanisms to be acutely aware of when your own emotional meter is close to reaching overload and then hold back or remove yourself from the situation is necessary.

Remind yourself that, as a Highly Sensitive Person, that you're not broken and there's actually nothing wrong with you. It's the way that you were born and also, you're not alone in dealing with this unique gift. You happen to be only one of between 15% and 20% of the world's total population and that's a pretty big number.

Give yourself time to get in touch with your emotional intelligence side. The greater the number of skills you're able to master, the more it's going to assist you in overcoming your anxiety, stress, and overstimulation. You'll be able to put things into perspective, which is actually a trait that you already possess—you may just need to put it into practice so that you can learn to master it as a skill.

There's definitely a place for Highly Sensitive Persons in this great big, noisy world that we live in. Whether you have always been aware that you are a Highly Sensitive Person, or whether this is something brand new to you and this is the first time that you're learning about it, once you embrace it, it will feel as though you are coming home after a long trip. You will feel it like a warm embrace when you need to be comforted. All of a sudden, there will be many things that will begin to make sense to you in your life.

If you have spent most of your life not quite knowing where you fit in, or whether you belong here or not, the answer is a resounding "yes, you do belong!" You are definitely needed and definitely necessary. The rest of the world needs you to show them how to take time to stop, pause, and reflect, before making their next moves.

This is one of your core traits and characteristics as an HSP. Don't be afraid to share your natural gifts and talents with the world. Don't be too hard on yourself either, if you feel like you are falling short of your own expectations. There is much for you to experience in the world. There are many individuals who desperately need the kindness and gentleness of character that you have to offer. What's most important though, is that you remember to show the same level of kindness to yourself. Don't be afraid to practice the four emotional intelligence strategies of self-awareness, self-management, social awareness, and social management as you move forward through your life as an HSP.

Here we have a great deal of information crammed into one single book in an attempt to make your life easier and more fulfilling. It is my recommendation that you don't take this information lightly or at face value. At this point, you may still have several questions about HSPs. Go back through each of the chapters and reread them for clarity. Whether you're looking for information on Highly Sensitive Persons for yourself, a loved one, or someone you work with, being armed with the information and insights contained on these pages is a really great starting point.

If you are, or suspect that you may be, an HSP, I suggest that you specifically go back through each of those chapters that resonates with you. After all, this is not the end of your journey as an HSP, or as a parent of an HSC. There is always much knowledge to be gained from material such as this. Above all, please be kind to yourself. I hope that this has given you, the HSP, more insight into who you are, and the wonderful gifts you have brought with you into this world.

Feel free to live your very best life, now that you've been given all the tools to do so. This may mean that you may need to refer back to certain chapters in this book again from time to time. That's completely fine. There are specific patterns that you can follow and introduce into your daily life that will help you to exist in such a way that you have a better grasp on your emotions. You'll be able to assess situations even quicker, but with greater accuracy. Emotional intelligence can make you more resilient in managing your response to emotions that you experience as you navigate your life. These are life skills that you can master and apply strategically whenever necessary.

As an author, I always appreciate receiving feedback, so that I know how I may continue to deliver high-quality information. If you have enjoyed this book, please leave a review on Amazon.

References

Andersen, N. (2018, July 23). *20 Self-Care ideas for highly sensitive people*. Highly Sensitive Refuge. https://highlysensitiverefuge.com/self-care-ideas-for-highly-sensitive-people/

Aron, E. (2016). *The highly sensitive person in love : understanding and managing relationships when the world overwhelms you*. Harmony Books.

Aron, E. (2020). *Highly Sensitive Person : How to thrive when the world overwhelms you*. Citadel Pr.

Aron, E. N. (2018, June 7). *New research on sensory processing sensitivity (SPS)*. Psychology Today. https://www.psychologytoday.com/us/blog/the-highly-sensitive-person/201806/new-research-sensory-processing-sensitivity-sps

Birch, J. (2019, July 24). *The 4 distinguishing traits of highly sensitive people who "just have a lot of feelings."* Well+Good. https://www.wellandgood.com/highly-sensitive-person/

Bjelland, J. (n.d.). *Signs an infant might be highly sensitive*. Julie Bjelland. https://www.juliebjelland.com/hsp-blog/signs-an-infant-might-be-highly-sensitive

Bjelland, J. (2017, December 1). *What does sensory overload feel like for a highly sensitive person? By Julie Bjelland, LMFT*. Julie Bjelland. https://www.juliebjelland.com/hsp-blog/2017/12/1/what-does-sensory-overload-feel-like-for-a-highly-sensitive-person-by-julie-bjelland-lmft

Boterberg, S., & Warreyn, P. (2016). Making sense of it all: The impact of sensory processing sensitivity on daily functioning of children. *Personality and Individual Differences*, 92, 80–86. https://doi.org/10.1016/j.paid.2015.12.022

Boyle, N. (2019, September 25). *Emotional Intelligence: The secret to managing your stress | The Village Family Service Center.* Www.Thevillagefamily.org. https://www.thevillagefamily.org/content/emotional-intelligence-secret-managing-your-stress

Bradberry, T. (2016, August 30). *9 Signs you're a highly sensitive person.* Forbes. https://www.forbes.com/sites/travisbradberry/2016/08/30/9-signs-youre-a-highly-sensitive-person/

Bradberry, T., & Greaves, J. (2009). *Emotional intelligence 2.0.* Talentsmart.

BrainyQuote. (n.d.). *Overload quotes.* BrainyQuote. https://www.brainyquote.com/topics/overload-quotes

Brindis. (2020, January 30). *Introduction to Emotional Intelligence | Brindis.* Brindis.co.uk. https://brindis.co.uk/introduction-to-emotional-intelligence/

Brooks, H. (2020, June 29). *19 Ways being a highly sensitive person affects your love life.* IntrovertDear.com. https://introvertdear.com/news/highly-sensitive-person-relationships-affects/

Callarman, S. (2020, June 8). *The Emotional Intelligence of highly sensitive people.* Highly Sensitive Refuge. https://highlysensitiverefuge.com/emotional-intelligence/

Campbell, S. (2015, April 23). *8 Advantages highly sensitive people bring to business.* Entrepreneur. https://www.entrepreneur.com/article/245293

Cherry, K., & Lehman, S. (2020, June 3). *How emotionally intelligent are you?* Verywell Mind. https://www.verywellmind.com/whati-is-emotional-intelligence-2795423

Davies, A. (2019, October 14). *This is what overstimulation feels like for HSPs*. Highly Sensitive Refuge. https://highlysensitiverefuge.com/what-overstimulation-feels-like/

Davies, D. (2019, March 4). *Is your child an orchid or a dandelion? Unlocking the science of sensitive kids*. NPR.org. https://www.npr.org/sections/health-shots/2019/03/04/699979387/is-your-child-an-orchid-or-a-dandelion-unlocking-the-science-of-sensitive-kids

Eanes, R. (n.d.). *Six things an orchid child needs to bloom*. Creative Child Magazine. https://www.creativechild.com/articles/view/six-things-an-orchid-child-needs-to-bloom

Expansive Heart. (n.d.). *How Highly Sensitive People Can Manage Anxiety*. Expansive Heart Psychotherapy. https://www.expansiveheart.com/blog/highly-sensitive-anxiety

Falkenstein, T. (2019, October 17). *How to deal with overstimulation*. Psychology Today. https://www.psychologytoday.com/us/blog/the-highly-sensitive-man/201910/how-deal-overstimulation

Fraga, J. (2018, August 28). *Being "Highly Sensitive" is a real trait. Here's what it feels like*. Healthline. https://www.healthline.com/health/mental-health/what-its-like-highly-sensitive-person-hsp

Granneman, J. (2019a, December 2). *14 Things highly sensitive people absolutely need to be happy*. Highly Sensitive Refuge. https://highlysensitiverefuge.com/things-highly-sensitive-people-need-happy/

Granneman, J. (2019b, December 13). *21 Signs you're a highly sensitive person*. Highly Sensitive Refuge. https://highlysensitiverefuge.com/highly-sensitive-person-signs/

Greven, C. U., Lionetti, F., Booth, C., Aron, E. N., Fox, E., Schendan, H. E., Pluess, M., Bruining, H., Acevedo, B., Bijttebier, P., & Homberg, J. (2019). Sensory Processing Sensitivity in the context of Environmental Sensitivity: A critical review and development of research agenda. *Neuroscience & Biobehavioral Reviews*, *98*, 287–305. https://doi.org/10.1016/j.neubiorev.2019.01.009

Grimen, H. L., & Diseth, Å. (2016). Sensory processing sensitivity. *Comprehensive Psychology*, *5*, 216522281666007. https://doi.org/10.1177/2165222816660077

Houston, E. (2019, August). *The importance of Emotional Intelligence (including EI quotes)*. PositivePsychology.com. https://positivepsychology.com/importance-of-emotional-intelligence/

Hulsmann, E. (2019, April 8). *7 Secret benefits of being a highly sensitive person*. Highly Sensitive Refuge. https://highlysensitiverefuge.com/benefits-highly-sensitive-person/

Jagiellowicz, J. (2019, December 30). *Help for anxiety, depression, negative thoughts*. Highly Sensitive Society. https://highlysensitivesociety.com/blog/tips-to-fight-stress-anxiety-depression-negative-thoughts

Jane. (n.d.). *20 Quotes for the highly sensitive woman*. www.habitsforwellbeing.com. https://habitsforwellbeing.com/20-quotes-for-the-highly-sensitive-woman/

Leonard, E. (2020, February 9). *The interplay between high EQ and anxiety*. Psychology Today. https://www.psychologytoday.com/za/blog/peaceful-parenting/202002/the-interplay-between-high-eq-and-anxiety

Lillarose, P. (2019, August 10). *10 Signs you're a "Highly Sensitive Person."* YourTango. https://www.yourtango.com/experts/pernilla-lillarose/signs-highly-sensitive-person-with-high-emotional-intelligence

Mind Tools. (n.d.). *Managing Highly Sensitive People: – Valuing quiet time.* www.Mindtools.com. https://www.mindtools.com/pages/article/managing-highly-sensitive-people.htm

Morin, A., & Lockhart, A.-L. T. (2020, September 17). *How to parent a sensitive child live in a less than sensitive world.* Verywell Family. https://www.verywellfamily.com/parenting-a-sensitive-child-8-discipline-strategies-1094942

Nerenberg, J. (2020, March 27). *How to deal with sensory overload as a sensitive person.* Greater Good. https://greatergood.berkeley.edu/article/item/how_to_deal_with_sensory_overload_as_a_sensitive_person

Petsinis, L. (2019, February 1). *10 Things you should know about being in a relationship with an HSP.* Highly Sensitive Refuge. https://highlysensitiverefuge.com/hsp-relationship-you-should-know/

Pluess, M., Assary, E., Lionetti, F., Lester, K. J., Krapohl, E., Aron, E. N., & Aron, A. (2018). Environmental sensitivity in children: Development of the Highly Sensitive Child Scale and identification of sensitivity groups. *Developmental Psychology, 54*(1), 51–70. https://doi.org/10.1037/dev0000406

Riopel, L. (2019, March 12). *Key names in Emotional Intelligence research.* PositivePsychology.com. https://positivepsychology.com/emotional-intelligence-goleman-research/

RocheMartin. (2019). *50 Tips for improving your emotional intelligence*. Rochemartin.com. https://www.rochemartin.com/blog/50-tips-improving-emotional-intelligence/

Salovey, P., & Mayer, J. D. (1990). Emotional Intelligence. *Imagination, Cognition and Personality*, 9(3), 185–211. https://doi.org/10.2190/dugg-p24e-52wk-6cdg

Schouten, B. (2019, May 22). *How to increase your EQ as an HSP (Highly Sensitive Person)*. www.2beinbalance.com. https://www.2beinbalance.com/How-to-increase-your-EQ-as-an-HSP-Highly-Sensitive-Person

Scott, E., & Gans, S. (2020, September 18). *Highly Sensitive Person traits that create more stress*. Verywell Mind. https://www.verywellmind.com/highly-sensitive-persons-traits-that-create-more-stress-4126393

Stewart, K. (2019, Autumn 2019). *5 Different types of Highly Sensitive People – Psych2Go*. www.psych2go.net. https://psych2go.net/5-different-types-of-highly-sensitive-people/

Stewart, L. (2019, April 22). *The no. 1 thing that relieves my anxiety as a highly sensitive person*. Highly Sensitive Refuge. https://highlysensitiverefuge.com/anxiety-highly-sensitive-person/

Tartakovsky, M. (2012, May 13). *10 Tips for highly sensitive people*. Psych Central. https://psychcentral.com/blog/10-tips-for-highly-sensitive-people#1

The Power of Ideas. (2019, July 14). *10 Types of highly sensitive people (and how you can protect yourself if you are one)*. Ideapod. https://ideapod.com/10-types-highly-sensitive-people-can-protect-one/

Tredgold, G. (2016, August 4). *55 Inspiring quotes that show the power of Emotional Intelligence*. Inc.com; Inc. https://www.inc.com/gordon-tredgold/55-inspiring-quotes-that-show-the-importance-of-emotional-intelligence.html

Ward, D. (2018, February 2). *The HSP relationship dilemma.* Psychology Today. https://www.psychologytoday.com/za/blog/sense-and-sensitivity/201802/the-hsp-relationship-dilemma

Wilding, M. (2019, December 9). How to make hypersensitivity your strongest skill at work. *Quartz.* https://qz.com/work/1762183/how-to-stop-overthinking-if-youre-a-highly-sensitive-person/

Wilding, M. (2020, November 5). *14 Ways to tell if you're a Highly Sensitive Person.* Melody Wilding. https://melodywilding.com/highly-sensitive-person-how-to-know/

Young, E. (2016, June 24). *Science may explain why some people have deeply sensitive personalities.* Quartz. https://qz.com/708934/science-may-explain-why-some-people-have-deeply-sensitive-personalities/

Zeff, T. (2004). *The highly sensitive person's survival guide: essential skills for living well in an overstimulating world.* New Harbinger.

Printed in Great Britain
by Amazon